THE LIFE OF ST. MALACHY OF ARMAGH

THE LIFE OF ST. MALACHY OF ARMAGH

St. Bernard of Clairvaux

TAN Books
Gastonia, North Carolina

This edition of *The Life of St. Malachy of Armagh* is from *St Bernard of Clairvaux's Life of St Malachy of Armagh* by H. J. Lawlor D.D., Litt.D. published by The Macmillan Company, London, New York and Richard Clay & Sons, Limited, Brunswick St., Stamford St., S.E. 1, and Bungay, Suffolk in 1920. It was retypeset and published in 2025 by TAN Books.

Cover design by Caroline Green

ISBN: 978-1-5051-3575-6
Kindle ISBN: 978-1-5051-3577-0
ePUB ISBN: 978-1-5051-3576-3

Published in the United States by
TAN Books
PO Box 269
Gastonia, NC 28053
www.TANBooks.com

Printed in the United States of America

Contents

Preface

1. It is indeed always worth while to portray the illustrious lives of the saints, that they may serve as a mirror and an example, and give, as it were, a relish to the life of men on earth. For by this means in some sort they *live* among us, even *after death*,[1] and many of those who *are dead while they live*[2] are challenged and recalled by them to true life. But now especially is there need for it because holiness is rare, and it is plain that our age is lacking in men. So greatly, in truth, do we perceive that lack to have increased in our day that none can doubt that we are smitten by that saying, *Because iniquity shall abound the love of many shall wax cold*;[3] and, as I suppose, he has come or is at hand of whom it is written,

1 Ecclus. xlviii. 12 (vg.).

2 1 Tim. v. 6. Cp. Rev. iii. 1.

3 Matt. xxiv. 12.

Want shall go before his face.[4] If I mistake not, Antichrist is he whom famine and sterility of all good both precedes and accompanies. Whether therefore it is the herald of one now present or the harbinger of one who shall come immediately, the *want* is evident. I speak not of the crowd, I speak not of the vile multitude of *the children of this world*:[5] I would have you lift up your eyes upon the very *pillars*[6] of the Church. Whom can you show me, even of the number of those who seem to be *given for a light to the Gentiles,*[7] that in his lofty station is not rather a smoking wick than a blazing lamp? And, says One, *if the light that is in thee be darkness, how great is that darkness*![8] Unless perchance, which I do not believe, you will say that they shine who *suppose that gain is godliness*;[9] who in the Lord's inheritance *seek not the things which are* the Lord's, but rather *their own.*[10] Why do I say *their own*? He would be perfect and holy, even while he seeks his own and retains his own, who

4 Job xli. 22 (vg.).
5 Luke xvi. 8.
6 Gal. ii. 9.
7 Isa. xlix. 6.
8 Matt. vi. 23.
9 1 Tim. vi. 5.
10 Phil. ii. 21; 1 Cor. xiii. 5.

should restrain his heart and hands from the things of others. But let him remember, who seems to himself to have advanced perhaps thus far, that the same degree of holiness is demanded even of a gentile.[11] Are not *soldiers* bidden to *be content with their wages* that they may be saved?[12] But it is a great thing for a doctor of the Church if he be as one of the soldiers; or, *if*, in truth (as the prophet speaks to their reproach), *it be as with the people so with the priest.*[13] Hideous! Is it so indeed? Is he rightly to be esteemed highest who, falling from the highest rank can scarce cleave to the lowest, that he be not engulfed in the abyss? Yet how rare is even such a man among the clergy! Whom, likewise, do you give me who is content with necessaries, who despises superfluities? Yet the law has been enjoined beforehand by the Apostles on the successors of the Apostles, *Having* food *and* raiment, *let us be therewith content.*[14] Where is this rule? We see it in books, but not in men. But you have [the saying] about the righteous man, that *the law of his God is in his heart,*[15] not in a codex. Nor is that

---

11 Cp. Matt. v. 47.

12 Luke iii. 14.

13 Isa. xxiv. 2; Hos. iv. 9 (inexact quotation).

14 1 Tim. vi. 8 (inexact quotation).

15 Ps. xxxvii. 31.

the standard of perfection. The perfect man is ready to forgo even necessaries. But that is beside the mark. Would that some limit were set on superfluous things! Would that our desires were not infinite! But what? Perhaps you might find one who can achieve this. It would indeed be difficult; but [if we find him] see what we have done. We were seeking for a very good man, a deliverer of many; and lo, we have labour to discover one who can save himself. The very good man today is one who is not utterly bad.

2. Wherefore, *since the godly man has ceased*[16] from the earth, it seems to me that I do not employ myself to no purpose when I recall to our midst, from among those *who were redeemed from the earth*,[17] Bishop Malachy, a man truly holy, and a man, too, of our own time, of singular wisdom and virtue. *He was a burning and a shining light*;[18] and it has not been quenched, but only removed. Who would with good right be angry with me if I move it back again? Yes indeed, neither the men of my own age, nor any succeeding generation should be wanting in gratitude to me if by my pen I

16 Ps. xii. 1.

17 Rev. xiv. 3.

18 John v. 35.

recall one whom the course of nature has borne away; if I restore to the world one *of whom the world was not worthy*;[19] if I preserve for the memory of men one *whose memory may be blessed*[20] to all who shall deign to read; if while I rouse my sleeping friend, *the voice of the turtle be heard in our land*[21] saying, *Lo, I am with you always, even unto the end of the world.*[22] Then again, he was buried among us; this duty is eminently ours. Nay, is it not mine, inasmuch as that holy man included me among his special friends, and in such regard that I may believe that I was second to none *in that respect of glory*?[23] Nor do I find that intercourse with holiness so eminent misses its reward; I have already received the first-fruits. He was near the end; nay, rather, near the beginning, according to the saying, *when a man hath finished then is he but at the beginning.*[24] I ran to him that *the blessing of him that was ready to* die might *come upon me.*[25] Already he could not move his other limbs;

---

19 Heb. xi. 38.

20 Ecclus. xlv. 1.

21 Cant. ii. 12.

22 Matt. xxviii. 20.

23 Apparently a confused reference to 2 Cor. iii. 10; xi. 17 (vg.).

24 Ecclus. xviii. 7 (inexact quotation).

25 Job xxix. 13.

but, mighty to give blessing, he raised his hands upon my head and blessed me. I have *inherited the blessing*;[26] how then can I be silent about him? Finally, you enjoin me to undertake this task, Abbot Congan, my reverend brother and sweet friend, and with you also (as you write from Ireland) *all* that *Church of the saints*[27] to which you belong. I obey with a will, the more so because you ask not panegyric but narrative. I shall endeavour that it may be chaste and clear, informing the devout, and not wearying the fastidious. At any rate the truth of my narrative is assured, since it has been communicated by you; and beyond doubt you assert nothing but things of which you have most certain information.

---

26 1 Pet. iii. 9.

27 Ecclus. xxxi. 11 (vg.).

Chapter I

The early life of Malachy. Having been admitted to Holy Orders he associates with Malchus.

1. Our Malachy, born in Ireland, of a barbarous people, was brought up there, and there received his education. But from the barbarism of his birth he contracted no taint, any more than the fishes of the sea from their native salt. But how delightful to reflect, that uncultured barbarism should have produced for us so worthy *a fellow-citizen with the saints and member of the household of God.*[28] He who brings *honey out of the rock and oil out of the flinty rock*[29] Himself did this. His parents, however, were great both by descent and in power, *like unto the name of the great men that are in the earth.*[30] Moreover his mother, more noble in mind than in blood, took pains, *in the very beginning of his*

28 Eph. ii. 19.

29 Deut. xxxii. 13.

30 2 Sam. vii. 9.

ways,[31] *to show* to her child *the ways of life*,[32] esteeming this knowledge of more value to him than the empty knowledge of the learning of this world. For both, however, he had aptitude in proportion to his age. In the schools *he was taught* learning, at home *the fear of the Lord*,[33] and by daily progress he duly responded to both teacher and mother. For indeed he was endowed from the first with a *good spirit*,[34] in virtue of which he was a docile boy and very lovable, wonderfully gracious to all in all things. But he was [now] drinking, instead of milk from the breast of a mother, *the waters of saving wisdom*,[35] and day by day he was increasing in discretion. In discretion, shall I say, or in holiness? If I say both, I shall not regret it, *for I should say the truth*.[36] He behaved as an old man, a boy in years without a boy's playfulness. And when because of this he was regarded with reverence and astonishment by all, he was not found on that account, as commonly happens, more arrogant, but rather quiet and subdued in

31 Prov. viii. 22.

32 Ps. xvi. 11.

33 Ps. xxxiv. 11.

34 Neh. ix. 20; Ps. cxliii. 10.

35 Ecclus. xv. 2, 3 (vg.).

36 2 Cor. xii. 6.

all meekness.[37] Not impatient of rule, not shunning discipline, not averse from reading, not, therefore, eager for games—so especially dear to the heart of boys of that age. *And he advanced beyond all of his own age*[38] in that learning, at least, which suited his years. For in discipline of morals and advance in virtues in a short time he even outshone *all his instructors*.[39] His *unction*,[40] however, rather than his mother, was his teacher. Urged by it he exercised himself not slothfully also in divine things, to seek solitude, *to anticipate vigils*,[41] to *meditate in the law*,[42] to eat sparingly, to pray frequently, and (because on account of his studies he had not leisure to frequent the church, and from modesty would not) to *lift up holy hands everywhere*[43] to heaven; but only where it could be done secretly—for already he was careful to avoid vainglory, that poison of virtues.

2. There is a hamlet near the city in which the boy studied, whither his teacher was wont to go often,

---

37 Eph. iv. 2.
38 Gal. i. 14.
39 Ps. cxix. 99.
40 1 John ii. 20.
41 Ps. lxxvii. 4 (vg.).
42 Ps. i. 2.
43 1 Tim. ii. 8.

accompanied by him alone. When they were going there both together, as he related afterwards, he would *step back, stop a moment,* and standing behind his teacher, when he was not aware of it, *spread forth his hands toward heaven,*[44] and quickly send forth a prayer, as if it were a dart; and, thus dissembling, once more would follow the teacher. By such a pious trick the boy often deceived him who was his companion as well as teacher. It is not possible to mention all the qualities which adorned his earlier years with the hue of a good natural disposition; we must hasten to greater and more useful matters. One further incident, however, I relate because, in my judgement, it yielded a sign, not only of good, but also of great hope in the boy. Roused once on a time by the reputation of a certain teacher, famous in the studies which are called liberal, he went to him desiring to learn. For indeed he was now grasping after the last opportunities of boyhood, and was longing eagerly for such learning. But when he went into the house he saw the man playing with an awl, and with rapid strokes making furrows in the wall in some strange fashion. And shocked at the bare sight, because it smacked of levity, the serious boy dashed away from

44 1 Kings viii. 22, 54.

him, and did not care even to see him from that time forward. Thus, though an avid student of letters, as a lover of virtue he esteemed them lightly in comparison with that which was becoming. By such preliminary exercises the boy was being prepared for the conflict which awaited him in more advanced age; and already in his own person he was challenging the adversary. Such, then, was the boyhood of Malachy. Moreover he passed through his adolescence with like simplicity and purity; except that as *years* increased, there *increased* also for him *wisdom and favour with God and man.*[45]

3. From this time, that is, from his early adolescence, *what was in the man*[46] began to appear more plainly, and it came to be seen that *the grace of God which was in him was not in vain.*[47] For the *industrious young man,*[48] seeing how *the world lieth in wickedness,*[49] and considering what sort of spirit *he had received,* said within himself, "It is *not the spirit of this world.*[50] What have

---

45 Luke ii. 40, 52.

46 John ii. 25.

47 1 Cor. xv. 10.

48 1 Kings xi. 28.

49 1 John v. 19.

50 1 Cor. ii. 12.

the two in common?[51] One has no *communion* with the other any more than *light with darkness.*[52] But my spirit *is of God,* and *I know the things that are freely given me*[53] in it. From it I have innocence of life till now, from it the ornament of continence, from it hunger for *righteousness,*[54] from it also that *glory of mine,* by so much more secure because it is more secret, *the testimony of my conscience.*[55] None of these is safe for me under *the prince of this world.*[56] Then, *I have this treasure in an earthen vessel.*[57] I must take heed lest it should strike against something and be broken, and the *oil of gladness*[58] which I carry be poured out. And in truth it is most difficult not to strike *against something amid* the stones and rocks *of this* crooked and winding *way and life.* Must I thus in a moment lose together all *the blessings of goodness with which* I have been *prevented*[59] from the beginning? Rather do I resign them,

51 Cp. John ii. 4 (vg.).
52 2 Cor. vi. 14.
53 1 Cor. ii. 12.
54 Cp. Matt. v. 6.
55 2 Cor. i. 12 (vg.).
56 John xiv. 30, etc.
57 2 Cor. iv. 7.
58 Ps. xlv. 7.
59 Ps. xxi. 3.

and myself with them, to Him from whom they come. Yea, and I am His. I *lose my* very *soul*[60] for a time that I may not lose it for ever. And what I am and all that I have, where can they be as safe as in the hand of their Author? Who so concerned to preserve, so powerful to hold, so faithful to restore? He will preserve in safety. He will restore in good time. Without hesitation I give myself to serve Him by His gifts. I cannot lose aught of all that I spend on my labour of piety. Perchance I may even hope for some greater boon. He who gives freely is wont to repay with usury. So it is. He will even heap up and *increase virtue in my soul*."[61]

So he thought—and did; *knowing that* apart from deeds *the thoughts of man are vanity*.[62]

4. (3) There was a man in the city of Armagh, where Malachy was brought up—a holy man and of great austerity of life, a pitiless *castigator of his body*,[63] who had a cell near the church. In it he abode, *serving God*

---

60 Matt. x. 39.

61 Ps. cxxxviii. 3 (vg.).

62 Ps. xciv. 11.

63 1 Cor. ix. 27 (vg.).

with fastings and prayers day and night.[64] To this man Malachy betook himself to receive a rule of life from him, who had condemned himself while alive to such sepulture. And note his humility. From his earliest age he had had God as his teacher—there is no doubt of it—in the art of holiness; and behold, he became once more the disciple of a man, himself a man *meek and lowly in heart.*[65] If we did not know it, by this one deed he himself gave us proof of it. Let them read this who attempt to teach what they have not learned, *heaping to themselves* disciples,[66] though they have never been disciples, *blind leaders of the blind.*[67] Malachy, *taught of God,*[68] none the less sought a man to be his teacher, and that carefully and wisely. By what better method, I ask, could he both give and receive a proof of his progress? If the example of Malachy *is* for them *a very small thing,*[69] let them consider the action of Paul. Did not he judge that his *Gospel,* though he had *not received it*

---

64 Luke ii. 37.

65 Matt. xi. 29.

66 Cp. 2 Tim. iv. 3.

67 Matt. xv. 14.

68 Isa. liv. 13; John vi. 45.

69 1 Cor. iv. 3.

of man but from *Christ,*[70] *should be discussed* with men, *lest by any means he was running or had run in vain*?[71] Where he was not confident, neither am I. If any one be thus confident let him take heed lest it be not so much confidence as rashness. But these matters belong to another time.

5. Now, however, the rumour of what had happened went through the city, and it was universally stirred by this new and unexpected event. All were amazed, and wondered at his virtue, all the more because it was unusual in a rude people. You would see that then *thoughts were being revealed out of the hearts of many.*[72] The majority, considering the act from a human standpoint, were lamenting and grieving that a youth who was an object of love and delight to all had given himself up to such severe labours. Others, suspecting lightness on account of his age, doubted whether he would persevere, and feared a fall. Some, accusing him of rashness, were in fact highly indignant with him because he had undertaken a difficult task, beyond his age and strength, without consulting them. But without coun-

70 Gal. i. 11, 12.

71 Gal. ii. 2.

72 Luke ii. 35.

sel he did nothing; for he had counsel from the prophet who says, *It is good for a man that he bear the yoke in his youth*, and adds, *He sitteth alone and keepeth silence because he hath borne it upon him.*[73] The youth sat at the feet of Imar (for that was the man's name) and either *learned obedience*[74] or showed that he had learnt it. He sat as one that was at rest, as meek, as humble. *He sat and kept silence*, knowing, as the prophet says, that *silence is the ornament of righteousness.*[75] *He sat* as one that perseveres, *he was silent* as one that is modest, except that by that silence of his he was speaking, with holy David, in the ears of God: *I am a youth and despised, yet do not I forget thy precepts.*[76] And for a time *he sat alone*, because he had neither companion nor example; for who before Malachy even thought of attempting the most severe discipline inculcated by the man? It was held by all indeed to be wonderful, but not imitable. Malachy showed that it was imitable by the mere act of sitting and keeping silence. In a few days he had imitators not a few, stirred by his example. So

73 Lam. iii. 27, 28 (inexact quotation).

74 Heb. v. 8.

75 Isa. xxxii. 17 (vg.).

76 Ps. cxix. 141 (vg.).

he who at first *sat alone*[77] and the only son of his father, became now one of many, from being *the only-begotten*[78] became *the firstborn among many brethren.*[79] And as he was before them in conversion, so was he more sublime than they in conversation; and he who came before all, in the judgement of all was eminent above all in virtue. And he seemed both to his bishop and to his teacher, worthy to be promoted to the degree of deacon. *And they constrained him.*[80]

6. (4) From this time onwards the Levite of the Lord publicly girded himself to every work of piety, but more especially to those things in which there seemed some indignity. In fact it was his greatest care to attend to the burial of the dead poor, because that savoured not less of humility than of humanity. Nor did *temptation* fail to test our modern Tobit, and, as in the old story, it came from a woman,[81] or rather from the serpent through a woman.[82] His sister, abhorring the indig-

---

77 Lam. iii. 28.
78 John i. 14, 18.
79 Rom. viii. 29.
80 Luke xxiv. 29.
81 Tobit ii. 12 (vg.).
82 Cp. Gen. iii. 12 f.

nity (as it seemed to her) of his office, said: "What are you doing, madman? *Let the dead bury their dead.*"[83] And she attacked him daily with this *reproach.*[84] But he *answered the foolish* woman *according to her folly,*[85] "Wretched woman, you preserve the sound of the *pure word,*[86] but you are ignorant of its force." So he maintained with devotion, and exercised unweariedly the ministry which he had undertaken under compulsion. For that reason also they deemed that the office of the priesthood should be conferred upon him. And this was done. But when he was ordained priest he was about twenty-five years old. And if in both his ordinations the rule of the Canons seems to have been somewhat disregarded—as indeed does seem to have been the case, for he received the Levitical ministry before his twenty-fifth, and the dignity of the priesthood before his thirtieth year—it may well be ascribed to the zeal of the ordainer and the merits of him who was ordained. But for my part, I consider that such irregularity should neither be condemned in the case of a saint, nor deliberately claimed by him who is not a saint. Not content

83 Matt. viii. 22.
84 Tobit ii. 23 (vg.).
85 Prov. xxvi. 5.
86 Ps. xii. 6.

with this the bishop also committed to him his own authority *to sow the* holy *seed*[87] in a *nation* which was not *holy*,[88] and to give to a people rude and living *without law*,[89] the law of life and of discipline. He received the command with all alacrity, even as he was *fervent in spirit*,[90] not hoarding up his talents, but eager for profit from them.[91] And behold he began to *root out* with the hoe of the tongue, *to destroy*, *to scatter*,[92] day by day making *the crooked straight and the rough places plain*.[93] *He rejoiced as a giant to run* everywhere.[94] You might call him a consuming *fire* burning *the briers* of crimes.[95] You might call him *an axe* or *a mattock casting down*[96] evil plantings. He extirpated barbaric rites, he planted those of the Church. All out-worn superstitions (for not a few of them were discovered) he abolished, and,

87 Luke viii. 5.
88 1 Pet. ii. 9.
89 Rom. ii. 12.
90 Rom. xii. 11.
91 Cp. Matt. xxv. 24 ff.
92 Jer. i. 10 (vg.).
93 Isa. xl. 4.
94 Ps. xix. 5.
95 Cp. Isa. x. 17.
96 Ps. lxxiv. 6 (vg.).

wheresoever he found it, every sort of malign influence *sent by evil angels.*[97]

7. In fine whatsoever came to his notice which was irregular or unbecoming or perverse his *eye did not spare;*[98] but as the hail scatters the *untimely figs* from *the fig-trees,*[99] and as *the wind the dust from the face of the earth,*[100] so did he strive with all his might to drive out before his face and destroy entirely such things from his people. And in place of all these the most excellent legislator delivered the heavenly laws. He made regulations full of righteousness, full of moderation and integrity. Moreover in all churches he ordained the apostolic sanctions and the decrees of the holy fathers, and especially the customs of the holy Roman Church. Hence it is that to this day there is chanting and psalmody in them at the canonical hours after the fashion of the whole world. For there was no such thing before, not even in the city. He, however, had learnt singing in his youth, and soon he introduced song into his monastery, while as yet none in the city, nor in the whole

97 Ps. lxxviii. 49 (vg.: inexact quotation).

98 Ezek. v. 11, etc.

99 Cp. Rev. vi. 13.

100 Ps. i. 4 (vg.).

bishopric, could or would sing. Then Malachy instituted anew the most wholesome usage of Confession, the Sacrament of Confirmation, the Marriage contract—of all of which they were either ignorant or negligent. And let these serve as an example of the rest, for [here] and through the whole course of the history we omit much for the sake of brevity.

8. (5). Since he had a desire and a very great zeal for the honouring of the divine offices and the veneration of the sacraments, lest by chance he might ordain or teach anything concerning these matters otherwise than that which was in accordance with the rite of the universal Church, it came into his mind to visit Bishop Malchus, that he might give him fuller information on all points. He was *an old man, full of days*[101] and virtues, and *the wisdom of God was in him.*[102] He was of Irish nationality, but had lived in England in the habit and rule of a monk in the monastery of Winchester, from which he was promoted to be bishop in Lismore, a city of Munster, and one of the noblest of the cities of that kingdom. There so great grace was bestowed upon him from above that he was illustrious, not only for life and

101 Gen. xxxv. 29; 1 Chron. xxiii. 1; Job xlii. 16.

102 1 Kings iii. 28.

doctrine, but also for signs. Of these I set down two as examples, that it may be known to all what sort of preceptor Malachy had in the knowledge of holy things. He healed a boy, who was troubled with a mental disorder, one of those who are called lunatics, in the act of confirming him with the holy unction. This was so well known and certain that he soon made him porter of his house, and the boy lived in good health in that office till he reached manhood. He restored hearing to one who was deaf; in which miracle the deaf person acknowledged a wonderful fact, that when the saint put his fingers into his ears on either side he perceived that two things like little pigs came out of them. For these and other such deeds, his fame increased and he won a great name; so that Scots and Irish flowed together to him and he was reverenced by all as the one father of all.

When therefore Malachy, having received the blessing of Father Imar, and having been sent by the bishop, came to him, after a prosperous journey, he was kindly received by the old man; and he remained with him for somc years, in order that by staying so long he might draw fuller draughts from his aged breast, knowing that which is written, *With the ancient is wisdom.*[103] But I suppose that another cause of his long sojourn was that the great Foreseer of all things would have His servant Malachy become known to all in a place to which so many resorted, since he was to be useful to all. For he could not but be dear to those who knew him. In fact one thing happened in that period, by which in some measure he made manifest to men what had been known to God as being in him.

9. A conflict having taken place between the king of South Munster—which is the southern part of Ireland—and his brother, and the brother being victorious, the king, driven from his kingdom, sought refuge with Bishop Malchus. It was not, however, in order that with his help he should recover the kingdom; but rather the devout prince *gave place unto wrath*[104] and made a virtue of necessity, choosing to lead a private life. And when the bishop was preparing to receive the king with due honour, he declined it, saying that he preferred to be as one of those poor brothers who consorted with him, to lay aside his royal state, and to be content with the common poverty, rather to await the

103 Job xii. 12.

104 Rom. xii. 19.

will of God than to get back his kingdom by force; and that he would not for his earthly honour *shed man's blood*,[105] since it would *cry unto* God against him *from the ground*.[106] When he heard this the bishop rejoiced greatly, and with admiration for his devotion satisfied his desire. Why more? The king is given a poor house for his dwelling, Malachy for his teacher, bread with salt and water for his food. Moreover for dainties, the presence of Malachy, his life and doctrine, were sufficient for the king; so that he might say to him, *How sweet are thy words unto my taste, yea, sweeter than honey to my mouth*.[107] Besides, *every night he watered his couch with his tears*,[108] and also with a daily bath of cold water he quenched the burning lust for evil in his flesh. And the king prayed in the words of another king, *Look upon my affliction and my pain; and forgive all my sins*.[109] And *God did not turn away his prayer nor His mercy from him*.[110] *And his supplication was heard*,[111] although oth-

---

105 Gen. ix. 6.
106 Gen. iv. 10.
107 Ps. cxix. 103.
108 Ps. vi. 6 (vg.).
109 Ps. xxiv. 18.
110 Ps. lxvi. 20.
111 Ecclus. li. 11.

erwise than he had desired. For he was troubled about his soul; but God, the avenger of innocence, willing to show men *that there is a remainder for the man of peace,*[112] was preparing meanwhile *to execute a judgement for the oppressed,*[113] which was utterly beyond his hope. And God *stirred up the spirit* of a neighbouring *king:*[114] for Ireland is not one kingdom, but is divided into many. This king therefore seeing what had been done, was filled with wrath; and indignant, on the one hand, at the freedom of the raiders and the insolence of the proud, and on the other, pitying the desolation of the kingdom and the downfall of the king, he went down to the cell of the poor man; urged him to return, but did not succeed in persuading him. He was instant, nevertheless, pledged himself to help him, assured him that he need not doubt the result, promised that God would be with him, *whom all his adversaries would not be able to resist.*[115] He laid before him also the oppression of the poor and the devastation of his country; yet he prevailed not.

112 Ps. xxxvii. 37 (vg.).

113 Ps. cxlvi. 7.

114 2 Chron. xxxvi. 22.

115 Luke xxi. 15.

10. But when to these arguments were added the command of the bishop and the advice of Malachy—the two men on whom he wholly depended—at length, with difficulty, he consented. A king followed a king, and according to the word of the king, *as was the will in heaven*,[116] the marauders were driven out with absolute ease, and the man was led back to his own, with great rejoicing of his people, and was restored to his kingdom. From that time the king loved and always reverenced Malachy; so much the more because he had learned more fully in the holy man the things that were worthy of reverence and affection. For he could not be ignorant of the holiness of him with whom he had enjoyed so much intimacy in his adversity. Therefore he honoured him the more in his prosperity with constant acts of friendship, and faithful services, *and he heard him gladly, and when he heard him did many things*.[117] But enough of this. Nevertheless I suppose it was not without purpose that the Lord so magnified him then *before kings*,[118] but *he was a chosen vessel unto Him*, about *to bear His name before kings* and princes.[119]

116 1 Macc. iii. 60.

117 Mark vi. 20.

118 Ps. cxix. 46.

119 Acts ix. 15.

Chapter II

Malachy's pity for his deceased sister. He restores the Monastery of Bangor. His first Miracles.

11. (6). Meanwhile Malachy's sister, whom we mentioned before, died: and we must not pass over the visions which he saw about her. For the saint indeed abhorred her carnal life, and with such intensity that he vowed he would never see her alive in the flesh. But now that her flesh was destroyed his vow was also destroyed, and he began to see in spirit her whom in the body he would not see. One night he heard in a dream the voice of one saying to him that his sister was standing outside in the court, and that for thirty entire days she had tasted nothing; and when he awoke he soon understood the sort of food for want of which she was pining away. And when he had diligently considered the number of days which he had heard, he discovered that it went back to the time when he had ceased to offer the *living bread from heaven*[120] for her. Then, since

120 John vi. 51.

he hated not the soul of his sister but her sin, he began again the good practice which he had abandoned. And not in vain. Not long after she was seen by him to have come to the threshold of the church, but to be not yet able to enter; she appeared also in dark raiment. And when he persevered, taking care that on no single day she should be disappointed of the accustomed gift, he saw her a second time in whitish raiment, admitted indeed within the church, but not allowed to approach the altar. At last she was seen, a third time, gathered in the company of the white-robed, and *in bright clothing.*[121] You see, reader, how much *the effectual fervent prayer of a righteous man availeth.*[122] Truly *the kingdom of heaven suffereth violence and the violent take it by force.*[123] Does not the prayer of Malachy seem to you to have played the part as it were of a housebreaker to the heavenly gates, when a sinful woman obtained by the weapons of a brother what was denied to her own merits? This *violence*, good Jesus, Thou who *sufferest* dost exercise, strong and merciful *to save*,[124] *showing* mercy

121 Acts x. 30.
122 Jas. v. 16.
123 Matt. xi. 12.
124 Cp. Isa. lxiii. 1.

and *strength with thine arm*,[125] and preserving it in thy sacrament for *the saints which are in the earth*,[126] *unto the end of the world*.[127] Truly this sacrament is strong to *consume* sins,[128] to defeat opposing powers, to bring into heaven those who are returning from the earth.

12. (7). The Lord, indeed, was so preparing His beloved Malachy in the district of Lismore for the glory of His name. But those who had sent him, tolerating his absence no longer, recalled him by letters. When he was restored to his people, now better instructed in all that was necessary, behold *a work prepared* and kept by *God*[129] for Malachy. A rich and powerful man, who held the place of Bangor and its possessions, by inspiration of God immediately placed in his hand all that he had and himself as well. And he was his mother's brother. But kinship of spirit was of more value to Malachy than kinship of the flesh. The actual place also of Bangor, from which he received his name, the prince made over to him, that there he might build, or

125 Luke i. 51.
126 Ps. xvi. 3.
127 Matt. xxviii. 20.
128 Ps vii. 9 (vg.).
129 Eph. ii. 10 (vg.).

rather rebuild, a monastery. For indeed there had been formerly a very celebrated one under the first father, Comgall, which produced many thousands of monks, and was the head of many monasteries. A truly holy place it was and prolific of saints, *bringing forth* most abundant *fruit to God*,[130] so that one of the sons of that holy community, Lugaid by name, is said to have been the founder—himself alone—of a hundred monasteries. I mention this in order that the reader may infer from this one instance what an immense number of others there were. In fine, to such an extent did its shoots fill Ireland and Scotland that those verses of David seem to have sung beforehand especially of these times, *Thou visitest the earth and blessest it; thou makest it very plenteous. The river of God is full of water: thou preparest their corn, for so thou providest for the earth, blessing its rivers, multiplying its shoots. With its drops of rain shall it rejoice while it germinates*;[131] and in like manner the verses that follow. Nor was it only into the regions just mentioned, but also into foreign lands that those swarms of saints poured forth as though a *flood had risen*;[132] of whom one, St. Columbanus, came up to our

130 Rom. vii. 4.

131 Ps. lxv. 9, 10 (vg., inexact quotation).

132 Luke vi. 48.

Gallican parts, and built the monastery of Luxovium, and was *made there a great people.*[133] So great a people was it, they say, that the choirs succeeding one another in turn, the solemnities of the divine offices went on continuously, so that not a moment day or night was empty of praises.

13. (8) Enough has been said about the ancient glory of the monastery of Bangor. This, long ago destroyed by pirates, Malachy eagerly cherished on account of its remarkable and long-standing prestige, as though he were about to *replant a paradise*,[134] and because *many bodies of the saints slept* there.[135] For, not to speak of those which were *buried in peace*,[136] it is said that nine hundred persons were slain together in one day by pirates. Vast, indeed, were the possessions of that place; but Malachy, content with the holy place alone, resigned all the possessions and lands to another. For indeed from the time when the monastery was destroyed there was always someone to hold it with its possessions. For they were both appointed by election

133 Gen. xii. 2.

134 Gen. ii. 8.

135 Matt. xxvii. 52.

136 Ecclus. xliv. 14.

and were even called abbots, preserving in name but not in fact what had once been. And though many urged him not to alienate the possessions, but to retain the whole together for himself, this lover of poverty did not consent, but caused one to be elected, according to custom, to hold them; the place, as we have said, being retained for Malachy and his followers. And perhaps, as afterwards appeared, he would have been wiser to have kept it all; only he looked more to humility than to peace.

14. So, then, by the command of Father Imar, taking with him about ten brethren, he came to the place and began to build. And there, one day, when he himself was cutting with an axe, by chance one of the workmen, while he was brandishing the axe in the air, carelessly got into the place at which the blow was aimed, and it fell on his spine with as much force as Malachy could strike. He fell, and all ran to him supposing that he had received a death-wound or was dead. And indeed his tunic was *rent from the top to the bottom*,[137] but the man himself was found unhurt, the skin so very slightly grazed that scarcely a trace appeared

137 Matt. xxvii. 51.

on the surface. The man whom the axe had laid low, stood unharmed while the bystanders beheld him with amazement. Hence they became more eager, and were found readier for the work. And *this was the beginning of the miracles*[138] of Malachy. Moreover the oratory was finished in a few days, made of smoothed planks indeed, but closely and strongly fastened together—a Scotic work, not devoid of beauty. And thenceforward God was served in it as in the ancient days; that is, with similar devotion, though not with like numbers. Malachy presided over that place for some time, by the ordinance of Father Imar, being at once the ruler and the rule of the brethren. They read in his life how they should behave themselves, and he was their leader *in righteousness and holiness before God*;[139] save that besides the things appointed for the whole community he did many things of an exceptional kind, in which he still more was the leader of all, and none of the others was able to follow him to such difficult practices.

At that time and place a certain man was sick, and the devil stood by him and suggested in plain speech that he should never heed the admonitions of Malachy, but

138 John ii. 11.

139 Luke i. 75.

if he should enter his house, he should attack and kill him with a knife. And when this became known, those who ministered to him, the sick man himself informing them, brought word to Malachy and warned him. But he, seizing his accustomed weapons of prayer, boldly attacked his enemy, and put to flight both disease and demon. *But the* man's *name was Malchus.*[140] He is brother according to the flesh of our Christian, abbot of Mellifont. For both are still alive, now brothers yet more, in spirit. For when he was delivered, immediately he was not ungrateful, but in the same place, having *turned to the Lord,*[141] he changed both his habit and his mind. And the brethren knew that the evil one was envious of their prosperity; and they were edified and made more careful henceforth.

15. (9). At the same place he healed a cleric, named Michael, who was suffering from dysentery and despaired of, by sending him something from his table. A second time, when the same person was smitten with a very grave disorder, he cured him both in body and mind. And from that moment *he clave to* God[142] and

140 John xviii. 10.
141 Acts ix. 35.
142 2 Kings xviii. 6.

to Malachy His servant, fearing *lest a worse thing should come unto him*,[143] if once more he should be found ungrateful for so great a benefit and miracle. And at present, as we have heard, he presides over a monastery in the parts of Scotland; and this was the latest of all Malachy's foundations. Through such deeds of Malachy both his reputation and his community increased daily, and his name became great both within and without the monastery, though not greater than the fact. For indeed he dwelt there even after he was made bishop, for the place was near the city.

143 John v. 14.

Chapter III

St. Malachy becomes Bishop of Connor; he builds the Monastery of Iveragh.

16. (10). At that time an episcopal see was vacant, and had long been vacant, because Malachy would not assent: for they had elected him to it. But they persisted, and at length he yielded when their entreaties were enforced by the command of his teacher, together with that of the metropolitan. It was when he was just entering the thirtieth year of his age, that he was consecrated bishop and brought to Connor.

But when he began to administer his office, the man of God understood that he had been sent not to men but to beasts. Never before had he known the like, in whatever depth of barbarism; never had he found men so shameless in regard of morals, so dead in regard of rites, so impious in regard of faith, so barbarous in regard of laws, so stubborn in regard of discipline, so unclean in regard of life. They were Christians in name, in fact pagans. There was no giving of tithes or first-fruits;

no entry into lawful marriages, no making of confessions: nowhere could be found any who would either seek penance or impose it. Ministers of the altar were exceeding few. But indeed what need was there of more when even the few were almost in idleness and ease among the laity? There was no fruit which they could bring forth from their offices among a people so vile. For in the churches there was not heard the voice either of preacher or singer. What was *the athlete of the Lord* to do? He must either yield with shame or with danger fight. But he who recognized that he was *a shepherd and not a hireling*, elected to stand rather than to *flee*, prepared to *give his life for the sheep* if need be.[144] And although all were wolves and there were no sheep, the intrepid shepherd stood in the midst of the wolves, rich in all means by which he might make sheep out of wolves—admonishing in public, arguing in secret, weeping with one and another; accosting men now roughly, now gently, according as he saw it to be expedient for each. And in cases where these expedients failed he offered for them a *broken and a contrite heart*.[145] How often did he spend entire nights in vigil, holding out his hands in prayer! And when they would

144 John x. 11-13.

145 Ps. li. 17.

not come to the church he went to meet the unwilling ones *in the streets and in the broad ways*, and *going round about the city*, he eagerly *sought*[146] whom he might gain for Christ.

17. (11). But further afield also, none the less, he very frequently traversed country parts and towns with that holy band of disciples, who never left his side. He went and bestowed even on *the unthankful*[147] *their portion of* the heavenly *meat.*[148] Nor did he ride on a horse, but went afoot, in this also proving himself an apostolic man. Good Jesus, *how great things* thy warrior *suffered for Thy name's sake*[149] from *crime-stained children.*[150] How great things he endured for Thee from those very men to whom, and on whose behalf, he spoke good things. Who can worthily express with how great vexations he was harassed, with what insults he was assailed, with what unrighteous acts provoked,[151] how often he was faint with hunger, how often afflicted *with cold*

146 Cant. iii. 2; cp. Ps. lix. 6, 14; Luke xiv. 21.
147 Luke vi. 35.
148 Luke xii. 42.
149 Acts ix. 16.
150 Isa. i. 4 (vg.).
151 Cp. 2 Pet. ii. 7 f.

and nakedness?[152] Yet *with them that hated peace he was a peacemaker,*[153] *instant*, nevertheless, *in season, out of season.*[154] *Being defamed he intreated;*[155] when he was dealt with unrighteously he defended himself with the shield of patience and *overcame evil with good.*[156] Why should he not overcome? *He continued knocking,*[157] and according to the promise, at length, sometimes, *to him that knocked it was opened.*[158] How could that not follow which *the Truth*[159] had declared beforehand should follow? *The right hand of the Lord brought mighty things to pass,*[160] because the *mouth of the Lord spoke*[161] the truth. Hardness vanished, barbarity ceased; the *rebellious house*[162] began gradually to be appeased, gradually to admit reproof, *to receive discipline.*[163] Barbarous laws

152 2 Cor xi. 27.
153 Ps. cxx. 6, 7 (vg.).
154 2 Tim. iv. 2.
155 1 Cor. iv. 13.
156 Rom. xii. 21.
157 Acts xii. 16.
158 Matt. vii. 8; Luke xi. 10.
159 John xiv. 6.
160 Ps. cxviii. 15, 16.
161 Isa. i. 20.
162 Ezek. ii. 5, etc.
163 Lev. xxvi. 23 (vg.).

disappear, Roman laws are introduced; everywhere the ecclesiastical customs are received, their opposites are rejected; churches are rebuilt, a clergy is appointed in them; the solemnities of the sacraments are duly celebrated; confessions are made; congregations come to the church; the celebration of marriage graces those who live together. In fine, all things are so changed for the better that today the word which the Lord speaks by the prophet is applicable to that nation; *those who* before *were not my people are now my people.*[164]

18. (12). It happened after some years that the city was destroyed by the king of the northern part of Ireland; for *out of the north* all *evil breaks forth.*[165] And perhaps that evil was good for those who used it well. For who knows that God did not wish to destroy by such a scourge the ancient evils of His people? By a necessity so dire Malachy was compelled, and he retired with a crowd of his disciples. Nor was his retirement spent in idleness. It gave opportunity for building the monastery of Iveragh, Malachy going there with his brothers, in number one hundred and twenty. There King Cormac met him. He it was who at a former time driven

164 1 Pet. ii. 10, combined with Hos. ii. 24.

165 Jer. i. 14.

out of his kingdom, under the care of Malachy by the mercy of God received consolation; and that place was in his kingdom. The king rejoiced to see Malachy, placing at the disposal of him and those who were with him himself and all that he had—as one who was neither ungrateful nor unmindful of a benefit. Many beasts were immediately brought for the use of the brothers; much gold and silver was also supplied, with regal munificence, for the expense of the buildings. He himself also *was coming in and going out with them*,[166] busy and ready to serve—in attire a king, but in mind a disciple of Malachy. And the Lord *blessed* that place *for* Malachy's *sake*,[167] and in a short time he was made great in goods, possessions and persons. And there, as it were beginning anew, the burden of law and discipline which he laid on others he bore with greater zeal himself, their bishop and teacher. Himself, *in the order of his course*,[168] did duty as cook, himself served the brothers while they sat at meat.[169] Among the brothers who succeeded one another in singing or reading in church he did not suffer himself to be passed over, but strenu-

166 Acts ix. 28 (inexact quotation).

167 Gen. xxx. 27.

168 Luke i. 8.

169 Cp. Luke xii. 37; xxii. 27.

ously fulfilled the office in his place as one of them. He not only shared but took the lead in [the life] of holy poverty, being especially zealous for it *more abundantly than they all.*[170]

170 Cp. 1 Cor. xv. 10; 2 Cor. xi. 23.

Chapter IV

Being made Archbishop of Armagh, he suffers many troubles. Peace being made, from being Archbishop of Armagh he becomes Bishop of Down.

19. (12). Meanwhile it happened that Archbishop Cellach fell sick: he it was who ordained Malachy deacon, presbyter and bishop: and knowing that he was dying he made a sort of testament to the effect that Malachy ought to succeed him, because none seemed worthier to be bishop of the first see. This he gave in charge to those who were present, this he commanded to the absent, this to the two kings of Munster and to the magnates of the land he specially enjoined by the authority of St. Patrick. For from reverence and honour for him, as the apostle of that nation, who had converted the whole country to the faith, that see where he presided in life and rests in death has been held in so great veneration by all from the beginning, that not merely bishops and priests, and those who are of the clergy, but also all kings and princes are subject to the

metropolitan in all obedience, and he himself alone presides over all. But a very evil custom had developed, by the devilish ambition of certain powerful persons, that the holy see should be held by hereditary succession. For they suffered none to be bishops but those who were of their own tribe and family. And for no short time had the execrable succession lasted, for fifteen generations (as I may call them) had already passed in this wickedness. And to such a point had *an evil and adulterous generation*[171] established for itself this distorted right, rather this unrighteousness worthy of punishment by any sort of death, that although at times clerics failed of that blood, yet bishops never. In a word there had been already eight before Cellach, married men, and without orders, albeit men of letters. Hence, throughout the whole of Ireland, all that subversion of ecclesiastical discipline, that weakening of censure, that abandonment of religion of which we have spoken already; hence everywhere that substitution of raging barbarism for Christian meekness—yea, a sort of paganism brought in under the name of Christianity. For—a thing unheard of from the very beginning of the Christian faith—bishops were transferred

171 Matt. xii. 39; xvi. 4.

and multiplied, without order or reason, at the will of the metropolitan, so that one bishopric was not content with one bishop, but nearly every single church had its bishop. No wonder; for how could the members of so diseased a head be sound?

20. Cellach, greatly grieving for these and other like evils of his people—for he was a good and devout man—took all care to have Malachy as his successor, because he believed that by him this evilly rooted succession might be torn up, since he was dear to all, and one whom all were zealous to imitate, *and the Lord was with him.*[172] Nor was he deceived of his hope; for when he died Malachy was put into occupation in his room. But not soon nor easily. For behold there is one of the evil seed to seize the place—Murtough by name. For five years, relying on the secular power, this man fastened himself upon the church, not a bishop but a tyrant. For the wishes of the devout had rather supported the claim of Malachy. At last they urged him to undertake the burden according to the ordinance of Cellach. But he, who shunned every high office as nothing else than his downfall, thought that he had

172 1 Sam. iii. 19, etc.

found good ground of excuse, because at that time it was impossible that he should have a peaceful entry. All were eager for so holy a work and pressed him; especially the two bishops, Malchus and Gilbert, of whom the former was the elder of Lismore mentioned above, the second he who is said to have been the first to exercise the office of legate of the Apostolic See throughout the whole of Ireland. These, when three years had now passed in this presumption of Murtough and dissimulation of Malachy, tolerating no longer the adultery of the church and the dishonour of Christ, called together the bishops and princes of the land, and came, in one spirit, to Malachy, prepared to use force. But he refused at first; pleading the difficulty of the project, the numbers, strength and ambition of that noble stock, urging that it was a great venture for him, a poor man and of no account, to oppose himself to men so many, so great, of such sort, so deeply rooted, who now for well-nigh two hundred years had *held* as *by hereditary right the sanctuary of God*,[173] and now also had taken possession of it before him; that they could not be rooted out, not even at the cost of human life; that it was not to his advantage that *man's blood should be shed*[174] on

173 Ps. lxxxiii. 12 (vg.).

174 Gen. ix. 6.

his account; and lastly, that he was joined to another spouse whom *it was* not *lawful for him to put away.*[175]

21. (14). But when they persisted eagerly in the contrary opinion, and cried out that the *word had come forth from the Lord,*[176] and moreover ordered him with all authority to undertake the burden, and threatened him with an anathema, he said, "You are leading me to death, but I obey in the hope of martyrdom; yet on this condition, that if, as you expect, the enterprise has good success, and God frees his *heritage* from *those that are destroying* it,[177] all being then at length completed, and the church at peace, it may be lawful for me to return to my former spouse and friend, poverty, from which I am carried off, and to put in my place there another, if then one is found fit for it." Note, reader, the courage of the man and the purity of his purpose who, for Christ's name, neither sought honour nor dreaded death. What could be purer or what braver than this purpose, that after exposing himself to peril and labour he should yield to another the fruit—peace and security itself in the place of authority? And this

175 Matt. xix. 2; Mark x. 2.

176 Ezek. xxxiii. 30.

177 Jer. l. 11.

he does, retaining for himself according to agreement a free return to poverty when peace and freedom are restored to the church. When they gave the pledge, at length he assented to their will; or rather to the will of God, who, he remembered, had long foreshown to him this occurrence, at the fulfilment of which he was now grieved. For indeed when Cellach was already ailing there appeared to Malachy—far away and ignorant [of Cellach's condition]—a woman of great stature and reverend mien. When he inquired who she was, the answer was given that she was the wife of Cellach. And she gave him a pastoral staff which she held in her hand, and then disappeared. A few days later, Cellach, when he was dying, sent his staff to Malachy, indicating that he should succeed him: and when he saw it he recognized that it was the same which he had seen [in vision]. It was the remembrance of this vision which specially put Malachy in fear, lest if he still refused he might seem to *resist* the Divine *will*, which he had ignored long enough.[178] But he did not enter the city as long as that intruder lived, lest by such act it should happen that any one of those should die to whom he came rather to minister life. Thus for two years (for so

178 Rom. ix. 19.

long the other survived), living outside the town, he strenuously performed the episcopal office throughout the whole province.

22. (15). When that person, then, had been removed by sudden death, again one Niall [*Nigellus*] (in truth *nigerrimus*, very black) quickly took possession of the see. And in appointing him as his successor, Murtough, while he was still alive, *made provision for his life*:[179] he was going forth to be damned, but in the person of Niall he would go on adding to the works of damnation. For he also was of the damned race, a relative of Murtough. But the king and the bishops and faithful of the land nevertheless came together that they might bring in Malachy. And lo, there was an *assembly of the wicked*[180] to oppose them. A certain man of the sons of Belial, ready for *mischief, mighty in iniquity*,[181] who *knew the place* where they had decided *to come together*,[182] gathered many with him and secretly seized a neighbouring high hill opposite to it, intending, when they were engaged with other things, suddenly to rush

---

179 Josh. ix. 24 (vg.).

180 Ps. xxii. 16.

181 Ps. lii. 1 (vg.).

182 Cp. John xviii. 2 (vg.).

upon them unawares and *murder the innocent.*[183] For they had agreed to butcher the king also with the bishop, that there might be none to *avenge the righteous blood.*[184] The plan became known to Malachy, and he entered the church, which was close by, and lifted up his hands in prayer to the Lord. Lo, there came *clouds and darkness,*[185] yea also *dark waters and thick clouds of the skies*[186] *changed the day into night,*[187] *lightnings and thunderings*[188] and *an horrible spirit of tempests*[189] presaged the last day, *and all* the elements *threatened* speedy *death.*

23. But that you may know, reader, that it was the prayer of Malachy that roused the elements, the tempest fell upon those *who sought his life,*[190] the *dark whirlwind*[191] enveloped only those who had made ready *the works of*

183 Ps. x. 8.
184 Matt. xxiii. 35, combined with Rev. vi. 10; xix. 2.
185 Ps. xcvii. 2.
186 Ps. xviii. 11.
187 Amos v. 8 (vg.).
188 Rev. iv. 5.
189 Ps. xi. 6.
190 Exod. iv. 19; Matt. ii. 20, etc.
191 Job iii. 6 (vg.).

darkness.[192] Finally, he who was the leader of so great wickedness was struck by a thunderbolt and perished with three others, companions in death as they had been partners in crime; and the next day their bodies were found half-burnt and putrid, clinging to the branches of trees, each where the wind *had lifted him up and cast him down.*[193] Three others also were found half dead; the rest were all scattered in every direction. But, as for those who were with Malachy, though they were close to the place, the storm *touched them not at all, neither troubled them.* In that fact we find fresh proof of the truth of that saying, *The prayer of the righteous pierceth the heavens.*[194] It is also a new example of the ancient miracle, by which in former times, when all Egypt was in darkness, Israel alone remained in light, as the Scripture says, *Wheresoever Israel was there was light.*[195] In this connexion occurs to me also what holy Elijah did, at one time bringing clouds and rain from the ends of the earth,[196] at another, calling down fire

---

192 Rom. xiii. 12.

193 Ps. cii. 10.

194 Ecclus. xxxv. 16 (inexact quotation).

195 Exod. x. 23 (inexact quotation).

196 2 Kings xviii. 41 ff.; Jas. v. 18.

from heaven on the revilers.[197] And now in like manner *God is glorified in*[198] His servant Malachy.

24. (16). In the thirty-eighth year of his age, the usurper having been driven out, the poor man, Malachy, entered Armagh, pontiff and metropolitan of all Ireland. But when the king and the others who had brought him in returned home, he remained *in the hand of God*;[199] and there remained for him *without fightings, within fears.*[200] For, lo, the viperous brood, raging and crying out that it was disinherited, aroused itself in full strength, within and without, *against the Lord and against His Anointed.*[201] Moreover, Niall, seeing that flight was inevitable, took with him certain insignia of that see, to wit, the copy of the Gospels, which had belonged to blessed Patrick, and the staff covered with gold and adorned with most costly gems, which they call "the staff of Jesus," because the Lord himself (as report affirms) held it in His hands and fashioned it; which are deemed of the highest honour and sanctity

197 2 Kings i. 9-12.
198 John xiii. 31.
199 Wisd. iii. 1.
200 2 Cor. vii. 5.
201 Ps. ii. 2; Acts iv. 26.

in that nation. They are, in fact, very well known and celebrated among the tribes, and so revered by all, that he who is once seen to have them is held by the *foolish and unwise people*[202] to be their bishop. That man—a vagabond and another *Satan—went to and fro in the land and walked up and down in it,*[203] bearing round the holy insignia; and, displaying them everywhere, he was for their sake everywhere received, by them winning the minds of all to himself, and withdrawing as many as he could from Malachy. These things did he.

25. But there was a certain prince, of the more powerful of the unrighteous race, whom the king before he left the city, had compelled to swear that he would maintain peace with the bishop, taking from him, moreover, many hostages. Notwithstanding this, when the king left he entered the city, and took *counsel* with his kinsmen and friends *how they might take* the holy man *by subtlety and kill him; but they feared the people*;[204] and having conspired to slay Malachy[205] they fixed a place

---

202 Deut. xxxii. 6.

203 Job i. 6, 7; ii. 2.

204 Matt. xxvi. 4, combined with Luke xxii. 2.

205 Cp. Acts xxiii. 12 f.

and day, and a traitor *gave them a sign*.[206] On that very day, when the prelate was now celebrating the solemnity of Vespers in the church with the whole of the clergy and a multitude of the people, that worthless man sent him a message in *words of peace with subtlety*,[207] asking him that he would deign to come down to him, so that he might make peace. The bystanders answered that he should rather come to the bishop, and that the church was a more suitable place for establishing peace; for they foresaw guile. The messengers replied that this was not safe for the prince; that he feared for his head, and that he did not trust himself to the crowds who, some days before, had nearly killed him for the bishop's sake. As they were contending in this way, these saying that he should go, those that he should not go, the bishop, desiring peace and not afraid to die, said, "Brethren, let me imitate my Master.[208] I am a Christian to no purpose if I do not *follow* Christ.[209] Perhaps by humility I shall bend the tyrant; if not, yet I shall conquer by rendering, a shepherd to a sheep, a priest to a layman, that duty which he owed to me. You also, as far as in me lies,

206 Matt. xxvi. 48.

207 1 Macc. i. 30.

208 Cp. 1 Cor. xi. 1.

209 Matt. x. 38, etc.

I shall edify not a little by such an example. For what if I should chance to be killed? *I refuse not to die,*[210] in order that from me you may have an example of life. It behoves a bishop, as the prince of bishops says, not *to be lord over the clergy, but to become an example to the flock*[211]—no other example truly than that which we have received from Him *who humbled himself and became obedient unto death.*[212] Who will give me [the opportunity] to leave this [example] to [my] sons, sealed with my blood? Try, at any rate, whether your priest has worthily learnt from Christ not to fear death for Christ." And he arose and went his way, all weeping, and praying that he would not so greatly desire to die for Christ that he should leave desolate so great a flock of Christ.

26. (17). But as for him, *setting his whole hope* in the Lord,[213] he went with all speed accompanied only by three disciples who were *ready to die with him.*[214] *When he crossed the threshold* of the house and suddenly came

---

210 Acts xxv. 11.

211 1 Pet. v. 3 (vg., inexact quotation).

212 Phil. ii. 8.

213 Ps. lxxviii. 7.

214 Acts xxi. 13; John xi. 16.

into the midst of the armed men—himself protected by the *shield of faith*[215]—the *countenances* of them all *fell*,[216] for *dread fell upon them*,[217] so that the bishop could say, *Mine enemies which trouble me became weak and fell*.[218] This *word is true*.[219] You might see the victim standing, the slaughterers surrounding him on all sides, with weapons in their hands; and there was none to sacrifice him. You might suppose their arms were benumbed; for there was none to stretch out a hand. For even that one also, who seemed to be the head of the evil, rose up, not to assail him but to show him reverence. Where is the sign, O man, which you had given for the death of the pontiff? This is a sign rather of honour than death; this postpones, it does not hasten death. Wonderful result! They offer peace who had prepared slaughter. He cannot refuse it who had sought it at the risk of life. Therefore peace was made—a peace so firm that from that day the priest found his foe not merely appeased, but obedient, devoted. When they heard this, all the faithful rejoiced, not only because

215 Eph. vi. 16.

216 Gen. iv. 6.

217 Exod. xv. 16.

218 Ps. xxvii. 2 (vg.).

219 John iv. 37.

the innocent blood was saved in that day,[220] but because by the merits of Malachy the souls of many wrong-doers escaped to salvation. And fear took hold on all that were round about when they heard how God had laid low, with sudden power, those two of His enemies who seemed most ferocious and powerful *in their generation*:[221] I refer to him with whom we are now concerned, and the other of whom I spoke above. For in a wonderful manner He *took them* both—one terribly punished in the body, the other mercifully changed in heart—*in the devices that they had imagined*.[222]

27. These matters so accomplished, the bishop now began to dispose and order in the city all things pertaining to his ministry with entire freedom, but not without constant risk of his life. For though there was no one now who would harm him openly, yet the bishop had no place that was safe from plotters, and no time when he could be at ease; and armed men were appointed to guard him day and night, though he rather *trusted in the Lord*.[223] But his purpose was to

---

220 Dan. xiii. 62.

221 Luke xvi. 8.

222 Ps. x. 2.

223 Jer. xvii. 7, etc.

take action against the schismatic already mentioned, forasmuch as he was seducing many by means of the insignia which he carried about, persuading all that he ought to be bishop, and so stirring up the congregations against Malachy and the unity of the church. And thus he did; and without difficulty in a short time he so *hedged up* all *his ways*[224] *through the grace given unto him by the Lord,*[225] and which he had toward all, that that evil one was compelled to surrender, to return the insignia, and henceforth to be quiet in *all subjection.*[226] Thus Malachy, albeit through many perils and labours, prospered day by day and was strengthened, *abounding* more and more *in hope and the power of the Holy Ghost.*[227]

28. (18). And God swept away, not only those who did evil to Malachy, but also those who disparaged him. A certain man, for example, who was in favour with the princes and magnates, and even with the king himself, because he was a flatterer and garrulous and

224 Hos. ii. 6.
225 Rom. xii. 3; xv. 15, etc.
226 1 Tim. ii. 11.
227 Rom. xv. 13 (vg.).

mighty in tongue,[228] befriended Malachy's opponents in all things, and impudently maintained their contention. On the other hand, when the saint was present, he *withstood him to the face*,[229] and when he was absent he disparaged him. Moreover he accosted him rudely everywhere, and especially when he knew that he was engaged in the more frequented assemblies. But he was soon visited with a suitable reward of his impudent tongue. The evil-speaking tongue swelled, and *became putrid and worms swarmed* from it[230] and filled the whole blasphemous mouth. He vomited them forth incessantly for well-nigh seven days, and at length with them spued out his wretched soul.

29. Once when Malachy was speaking before the people and exhorting them, a certain unhappy woman dared to interrupt his discourse with evil cries, showing no respect to the priest *and the Spirit which spake*.[231] Now she was of the impious race; and having *breath in her nostrils* she vomited out blasphemies and insults against the saint, saying that he was a hypocrite, and

228 Ecclus. xxi. 7.

229 Gal. ii. 11.

230 Exod. xvi. 20 (vg., inexact quotation).

231 Acts vi. 10 (vg.).

an invader of the inheritance of another, and even reproaching him for his baldness. But he, modest and gentle as he was, *answered* her *nothing*;[232] but the Lord answered for him. The woman became insane by the judgement of the Lord, and crying out many times that she was being suffocated by Malachy, at length by a horrible death she expiated the sin of blasphemy. So this wretched woman, taking up against Malachy the reproach that had been made against Elisha,[233] found to her cost that he was indeed another Elisha.

30. Further, because on account of a certain pestilence which arose in the city, he had solemnly led out a multitude of the clergy and people with the memorial of the saints, neither is this to be passed over, that when Malachy prayed the pestilence immediately ceased. Thenceforward there was none to murmur against him, for those who were of the *seed of Canaan*[234] *said, Let us flee from the face of* Malachy, *for the Lord fighteth for him.*[235] But it was too late, for the wrath of the Lord, coming everywhere upon them, pursued them *even*

232 Mark xiv. 61.

233 2 Kings ii. 23.

234 Dan. xiii. 56.

235 Exod. xiv. 25.

unto destruction.[236] How, in a few days, *is their memorial perished with resounding noise;*[237] *how are they brought into desolation, they are consumed in a moment, they are punished for their iniquity.*[238] A great miracle today is the extinction of that generation, so quickly wrought, especially for those who knew their pride and power. And *many other signs truly*[239] were there by which God glorified His name and strengthened His servant amidst labours and dangers. Who can worthily recount them? Yet we do not omit them all, though we have not ability to describe all. But that the sequence of the narrative may not be interrupted we reserve to the end some that we propose to mention.

31. (19). So then Malachy, when within three years *a reward was rendered to the proud*[240] and liberty restored to the church, barbarism driven out and the customs of the Christian religion everywhere instituted anew, seeing that all things were at peace, began to think also of his own peace. And mindful of his design he appointed

---

236 Deut. vii. 2 (vg.).

237 Ps. ix. 6 (vg.).

238 Ps. lxxiii. 19.

239 John xx. 30.

240 Ps. xciv. 2.

in his own place Gelasius, a good man, and worthy of so great an honour, the clergy and people tacitly assenting, or rather supporting him because of the agreement. For apart from that it seemed altogether cruel. And when he had been consecrated and earnestly commended to the kings and princes, Malachy himself, renowned for miracles and triumphs, returned to his parish; but not to Connor. Hear the cause, which is worth relating. It is said that that diocese in ancient times had two episcopal sees, and that there were two bishoprics; an arrangement which seemed to Malachy preferable to the existing one. Hence those bishoprics which ambition had welded into one, Malachy divided again into two, yielding one part to another bishop and retaining the other for himself. And for this reason he did not come to Connor, because he had already ordained a bishop in it; but he betook himself to Down, separating the parishes *as in the days of old.*[241] O pure heart! O dove-like eye![242] He handed over to the new bishop the place which seemed better organized, which was held to be more important, the place in which he himself had sat. Where are they that fight about boundaries, carrying on perpetual hostilities against one another for

241 Isa. li. 9; Amos ix. 11.

242 Cp. Cant. i. 15; iv. i.; v. 12.

a single village? I know not if there is any class of men whom that ancient prophecy touches more than those: *They have ripped up the women with child of Gilead that they might enlarge their border.*[243] But this at another place.

32. When Malachy was made bishop of Down, immediately according to his custom he was at pains to take to himself from his sons, for his comfort, a convent of regular clerics. And lo, again he girds himself, as though a new recruit of Christ, for the spiritual conflict; again he puts on the *weapons* that are *mighty through God*,[244] the humility of holy poverty, the rigour of monastic discipline, the quietness of contemplation, continuance in prayer. But all these things for a long time he was able to maintain rather in will than in deed. For all men came to him; not only obscure persons, but also nobles and magnates, hastened to commit themselves to his wisdom and holiness for instruction and correction. And he himself meanwhile went about; *he went out to sow his seed*,[245] disposing and decreeing with all authority concerning ecclesiastical affairs, like

243 Amos i. 13.

244 2 Cor. x. 4.

245 Luke viii. 5.

one of the Apostles. And none *said unto him, By what authority doest thou these things?*[246] inasmuch as all *saw the miracles* and wonders *which* he did,[247] and because *where the Spirit of the Lord is, there is liberty.*[248]

---

246 Matt. xxi. 23; Mark xi. 28.
247 Acts viii. 6; John ii. 23.
248 2 Cor. iii. 17.

Chapter V

The Roman Pilgrimage: the Miracles which were wrought in it.

33. (20). It seemed to him, however, that one could not go on doing these things with sufficient security without the authority of the Apostolic See; and for that reason he determined to set out for Rome, and most of all because the metropolitan see still lacked, and from the beginning had lacked, the use of the pall, which is the fullness of honour. And it *seemed good in his eyes*[249] that the church for which he had laboured so much should acquire, by his zeal and labour, that privilege which hitherto it had not had. There was also another metropolitan see, which Cellach had constituted anew, though subject to the first see and to its archbishop as primate. For it also Malachy no less desired the pall, and that the prerogative which it had attained by the gift of Cellach should be confirmed by the authority of the Apostolic See. When his purpose became known it

249 1 Sam. xiv. 36, 40 (vg.).

displeased both the brothers and the magnates and people of the country; because all judged that they could not endure so long an absence of the loving father of them all, and because they feared he might die.

34. It happened meanwhile that his brother, Christian by name, died, *a good man, full of grace and* power.[250] He was a bishop second to Malachy in reputation, but in holiness of life and zeal for righteousness perhaps his equal. His departure made all the more afraid, and rendered a parting from Malachy more grievous. They said, in fact, that they would in no wise assent to the pilgrimage of their only protector, since *the whole land* would *be made desolate*[251] if in one moment it was bereaved of two such *pillars*.[252] Therefore all, with one voice, opposed him, and would have used force but that he threatened them with divine vengeance. They refused to desist, however, till the will of God on this matter should be asked by the casting of a lot. He forbade it: nevertheless they cast the lot, but thrice it was found to give an answer in favour of Malachy. For they were not content with one trial, so eager were they to

250 Acts vi. 8 (vg.), combined with Acts xi. 24.

251 Jer. xii. 11.

252 Gal. ii. 9.

retain him. Yielding at length they let him go, but not without *lamentation and weeping and great mourning.*[253] But that he should leave nothing imperfect he began to take measures by which he might *raise up the seed of his* dead *brother.*[254] And three of his disciples having been summoned to him he deliberated anxiously which should seem more worthy, or, in other words, more useful, for this work. And when he had scrutinized them one by one, he said, "Do you, Edan" (that was the name of one of them), "undertake the burden." And when he hesitated and wept, he proceeded, "Do not fear; for you have been designated to me by the Lord; for just now I saw in anticipation the gold ring with which you are to be espoused on your finger." He assented, and when he had been consecrated Malachy set out on his journey.

35. And when he had left Scotland and reached York, a priest, named Sycarus, *steadfastly beholding him*[255] recognized him. For though he had not seen his face before, because he *had the spirit of prophecy*[256] he had

253 Matt. ii. 18.

254 Deut. xxv. 5 (vg.).

255 Acts xiv. 9.

256 Rev. xix. 10.

received a revelation concerning him long ago. And now without hesitation he pointed him out with his finger to those who stood round him, saying, "*This is he of whom I had said* that from Ireland *there shall come*[257] a holy bishop who *knoweth the thoughts of man*."[258] So the *lamp* could not be hid *under a bushel*, for the Holy Spirit who *lighted* it[259] brought it forth by the mouth of Sycarus. For also many secret things concerning the affairs of him and his companions were told him by Sycarus, all of which he acknowledged to be or to have been. But when the companions of Malachy went on to inquire about their return, Sycarus immediately replied—and *the event afterwards proved the truth of the saying*[260]—that evidently very few of their number would return with the bishop. When they heard that they imagined that he apprehended death: but God fulfilled it in another way; for on his way back from the City he left some with us, and some in other places, to learn the rule of life; and so, *according to the word* of

257 John i. 30.

258 Ps. xciv. 11.

259 Matt. v. 15; Mark iv. 21; Luke xi. 33.

260 Gen. xli. 13 (vg.).

Sycarus,[261] he returned to his own country with very few companions. So much concerning Sycarus.

36. In the same city of York he was visited by a man of noble rank according to the standard of the world, Waltheof by name, then prior of the regular brothers at Kirkham, but now a monk, and father of the monks at Melrose, a monastery of our Order, who devoutly commended himself with humility to Malachy's prayers. And when he noticed that the bishop had many companions and few horses—for besides ministers and other clerks he had with him five presbyters, and only three horses—he offered him his own, on which he rode, saying that he regretted only one thing, that it was a pack-horse and a rough animal to ride. And he added, "I would have given it more willingly if it had been better; but, if you think it worth while, take it with you, such as it is." "And I," replied the bishop, "accept it the more willingly the more valueless you proclaim it, because nothing can be of no value to me which so precious a will offers;" and, turning to his companions, "Saddle this horse for me, for it is suitable for me, and will suffice for a long time." This done, he

261 2 Kings vi. 18, etc.

mounts. And at first he considered it rough, as it was, but afterwards, by a wonderful change, he found that it suited him well and ambled pleasantly. And that there might not *fall* on *the ground* any part of the word which he had spoken,[262] till the ninth year, the year in which he died, it did not fail him, and became an excellent and very valuable palfrey. And—that which made the miracle more evident to those that saw—from being nearly black it began to grow white, and after no long time there was scarcely a whiter horse to be found than it.

37. (21). To me also it was granted to see the man on that journey, and by the sight of him and by his word I was refreshed, and *I rejoiced as in all riches*;[263] and I, in turn, though a sinner, *found grace in his sight*[264] then, and from that time up to his death, as I said in the Preface. He also, deigning to turn aside to Clairvaux, when he saw the brothers was deeply moved; and they were not a little edified by his presence and his speech. So accepting the place and us, and gathering us into his inmost heart, he bade us farewell and departed. And

262 1 Sam. iii. 19. Cp. Matt. x. 29.

263 Ps. cxix. 14.

264 Gen. xxxiii. 10, etc.

crossing the Alps he came to Ivrea, a city of Italy, where he immediately healed the little son of his host who *was sick and ready to die.*[265]

38. Pope Innocent II., of happy memory, was then in the Apostolic See. He received him courteously, and displayed kindly pity for him on account of his long pilgrimage. And Malachy in the first place asked with many tears for that which he had fixed most deeply in his heart, that he might be allowed to live and die at Clairvaux, with the permission and blessing of the chief Pontiff. He sought this, not forgetful of the purpose for which he had come, but influenced by the longing for Clairvaux which he had brought with him. But he did not obtain his request, because the apostolic man decided that he should be employed to more profitable advantage. He was not, however, wholly disappointed of *his heart's desire,*[266] since it was granted him if not to live, at least to die there. He spent a whole month in the City, visiting the holy places and resorting to them for prayer. During that time the chief Pontiff made frequent and careful inquiry of him and those who were with him concerning the affairs of their country, the

265 Luke vii. 2.
266 Ps. xxi. 2.

morals of the people, the state of the churches, and the great things that God had wrought by him in the land. And when he was already preparing to return home the Pope committed his own authority to him, appointing him legate throughout the whole of Ireland. For Bishop Gilbert, who, as we have mentioned above, was then legate, had intimated to him that by reason of age and infirmity of body *he could no longer discharge the duties of the office.*[267] After this Malachy prayed that the constitution of the new metropolis should be confirmed, and that palls should be given him for both sees. The privilege of confirmation he soon received; "but regarding the palls," said the chief Pontiff, "more formal action must be taken. You must call together the bishops and clerks and the magnates of the land and hold a general council; and so with the assent and common desire of all ye shall demand the pall by persons of honest repute, and it shall be given you." Then he took his mitre from his own head, and placed it on Malachy's head, and more, he gave him the stole and maniple which he was accustomed to use in the offering; and saluting him with the kiss of peace he

---

267 Luke xvi. 2 (vg.).

dismissed him, strengthened with the apostolic blessing and authority.

39. And returning by Clairvaux he bestowed on us *a second* benediction.[268] And sighing deeply that it was not allowed him to remain as he longed to do, he said, "Meanwhile I pray you to keep these men for me, that they may learn from you what they may afterwards teach us." And he added, "They will be to us for a seed, *and in* this *seed shall the nations be blessed*,[269] even those nations which from ancient days have heard the name of monk, but have not seen a monk." And leaving four of his most intimate companions he departed: and they, when they were proved and found worthy, were made monks. After a time, when the saint was now in his own country, he sent others, and they were dealt with in like manner. And when they had been instructed for some time *and had applied their hearts unto wisdom*,[270] the holy brother Christian, who was one of themselves, was given to them to be their father, and we sent them out, adding from our own a sufficient number for an abbey. And this abbey *conceived and bare* five *daugh-*

268 Cp. 2 Cor. i. 15.

269 Gen. xxii. 18; xxvi. 4.

270 Ps. xc. 12.

ters,[271] and the seed being thus multiplied[272] the number of monks increases from day to day according to the desire and prophecy of Malachy. Now let us return to the order of the narrative.

40. (22). Malachy having set out from us had a prosperous journey through Scotland. And he found King David, who is still alive today, in one of his castles; and his son *was sick nigh unto death*.[273] And when Malachy entered the king's house he was honourably received by him and prevailed upon by humble entreaty *that he would heal his son*.[274] He sprinkled the youth with water which he had blessed, and *fastening his eyes upon him* said,[275] "Trust me, my son; you shall not die this time." He said this, and on the next day, according to his word, there followed the cure, and after the cure the joy of the father and the shouting and noise of the whole exulting family. The *rumour went forth*[276] to all, for what happened in the royal house and to the

271 1 Sam. ii. 21.
272 Cp. Gen. xxii. 17; xxvi. 4.
273 Phil. ii. 27 (inexact quotation).
274 2 John iv. 47.
275 Acts iii. 4.
276 Luke vii. 17.

king's son *could not be hid.*[277] And lo, everywhere there resounded *thanksgiving and the voice of praise*,[278] both for the salvation of their lord, and for the novelty of the miracle. This is Henry; for he still lives, the only son of his father, a brave and prudent knight, taking after his father as they say, in *following after righteousness*[279] and love of the truth. And both loved Malachy, as long as he lived, because he had recalled him from death. They asked him to remain some days; but he, shunning renown, was impatient of delay, and in the morning went on his way.

As he passed, therefore, through the village called Crug-gleton, a dumb girl met him. While he prayed *the string of her tongue was loosed and she spake plain.*[280]

Then he entered the village which they call St. Michael's Church, and before all the people cured a woman who was brought to him, mad and bound with cords; and when he had sent her away restored he went on.

277 Mark vii. 24.

278 Isa. li. 3 (vg.).

279 Rom. ix. 30, etc.

280 Mark vii. 35.

But when he came to Portus Lapasperi, he waited there for a passage some days; but the time of delay did not pass idly. In the interval an oratory is constructed of twigs woven into a hedge, he both giving directions and himself working. When it was finished he surrounded it with a wall, and blessed the enclosed space for a cemetery. The merits of him who blessed, the miracles, which are said to be wrought there frequently to this day, sufficiently declare.

41. Hence it came that they were in the habit of carrying thither from the neighbouring places those *that were* infirm and *diseased*, and *many* were healed.[281] A woman paralysed in all her limbs, brought thither on a waggon, returned home on foot, having waited only one night in the holy place, not in vain, for the mercy of the Lord.

Let these incidents—a few out of many—suffice with reference to that place; for now we must proceed with what remains.

---

281 Mark i. 32, 34.

Chapter VI

St. Malachy's Apostolic Labours, Praises and Miracles.

42. (23). Malachy embarked in a ship, and after a prosperous voyage landed at his monastery of Bangor, so that his first sons might receive the first *benefit.*[282] In what state of mind do you suppose they were when they received their father—and such a father—in good health from so long a journey? No wonder if their whole heart gave itself over to joy at his return, when swift rumour soon brought incredible gladness even to the tribes outside round about them. In fine, from the cities and castles and hamlets they ran to meet him, and wherever he turned he was received with *the joy of the whole land.*[283] But honour is not to his taste. He exercises his office as legate; many assemblies are held in many places, so that no region, or part of a region, may be defrauded of the fruit and advantage of his

---

282 2 Cor. i. 15.

283 Ps. xlviii. 2.

legation. He *sows beside all waters*;[284] there is not one who can escape from his sedulous care. Neither sex, nor age, nor condition, nor [religious] profession is held in account. Everywhere the saving seed is scattered, everywhere the heavenly trumpet sounds. He scours every place, everywhere he breaks in, with *the sword* of his tongue unsheathed *to execute vengeance upon the nations and punishments upon the peoples.*[285] The terror of him is *on them that do evil.*[286] He cries *unto the unrighteous, deal not unrighteously, and to the wicked, lift not up the horn.*[287] Religion is planted everywhere, is propagated, is tended. His *eyes are upon* them,[288] his care is for their necessities. In councils, which are everywhere held, the ancient traditions are revived, which, though their excellence was undisputed, had fallen into disuse by the negligence of the priests. And not only are the old restored, new customs are also devised; and whatsoever things he promulgated are accepted as though issued from heaven, are held fast, are committed to writing for a memorial to posterity. Why should we not believe

---

284 Isa. xxxii. 20.

285 Ps. cxlix. 6, 7.

286 Ps. xxxiv. 16; 1 Pet. iii. 12.

287 Ps. lxxv. 4 (vg.).

288 Ps. xxxiv. 15; 1 Pet. iii. 12.

those things were sent from heaven which so many heavenly miracles confirm? And that I may make what has been said credible, let me touch on some of these miracles in a few words. For who can enumerate all? Though I confess I had rather dwell on those things which can be imitated than on those which can only excite wonder.

43. (24). And in my judgement the first and greatest miracle that he exhibited was himself. For to say nothing of his *inner man*,[289] the beauty and strength and purity of which his habits and life sufficiently attested, he so bore himself even outwardly in a uniform and consistent manner, and that the most modest and becoming, that absolutely nothing appeared in him which could offend the beholders. And, indeed, *he who offends not in word, the same is a perfect man.*[290] But yet in Malachy, who, though he observed with unusual care, ever detected, I will not say an *idle word*,[291] but an idle nod? Who ever knew his hand or his foot to move without purpose? Yea, what was there that was not edifying in his gait, his mien, his bearing, his countenance?

---

289 Eph. iii. 16.

290 Jas. iii. 2.

291 Matt. xii. 36.

In fine, neither did sadness darken nor laughter turn to levity the joyousness of his countenance. Everything in him was under *discipline*, everything a mark *of virtue*, *a rule* of perfection. Always he was grave, but not austere. Relaxing at times, but never careless; neglecting nothing, though for a time ignoring many things. Quiet often, but by no means at any time idle. From the first day of his conversion to the last of his life, he lived without personal possessions. He had neither *menservants* nor *maidservants*,[292] nor villages nor hamlets, nor in fact any revenues, ecclesiastical or secular, even when he was a bishop. There was nothing whatever ordained or assigned for his episcopal mensa, by which the bishop might live; for he had not even a house of his own. But he was almost always going about all the parishes serving the Gospel,[293] and *living of the Gospel*,[294] as the Lord appointed for him when he said, *The labourer is worthy of his hire.*[295] Except that more frequently, *making the Gospel* itself *without charge*,[296] as a result of the labours of himself and his companions, he brought

292 Gen. xxxii. 5, etc.

293 Cp. Rom. i. 9.

294 1 Cor. ix. 14.

295 Luke x. 7.

296 1 Cor. ix. 18.

with him that by which he might sustain himself and *those who laboured with him in the work of the ministry.*[297] Further, if at times he had to rest he did so in the holy places which he himself had scattered through the whole of Ireland; but he conformed to the customs and observances of those with whom it pleased him to tarry, content with the common life and the common table. There was nought in his food, nought in his clothing, by which Malachy could be distinguished from the rest of the brethren; to such a degree, though he was *greatest,* did he *humble himself in all things.*[298]

44. Then, when he went out to preach, he was accompanied by others on foot, and on foot went he himself, the bishop and legate. That was the apostolic rule; and it is the more to be admired in Malachy because it is too rare in others. The true successor of the Apostles assuredly is he who does such things. But it is to be observed how he *divides the inheritance with his brothers,*[299] equally descendants of the Apostles. They *lord it among the clergy;*[300] he, *though he was free from all men,*

297 Phil. iv. 3 combined with Eph. iv 12; cp. Acts xx. 34.

298 Matt. xviii. 4, combined with Ecclus. iii. 20.

299 Luke xii. 13.

300 1 Pet. v. 3 (vg.).

made himself the servant of all.[301] They either do not preach the Gospel and yet eat, or preach the Gospel in order that they may eat; Malachy, imitating Paul, eats that he may preach the Gospel. They *suppose that* arrogance and *gain are godliness*;[302] Malachy claims for himself by inheritance labour and a load. They believe themselves happy if they *enlarge their borders*;[303] Malachy glories in enlarging charity.[304] They *gather into barns*[305] and fill the wine-jars, that they may load their tables; Malachy collects [men] into deserts and solitudes that he may fill the heavens. They, though they receive tithes and first-fruits and oblations, besides customs and tributes by the gift of Cæsar and countless other revenues, nevertheless *take thought what they shall eat or what they shall drink*;[306] Malachy *having nothing* of such things, yet *makes many rich*[307] out of the storehouse of faith. Of their desire and anxiety there is no end; Malachy, desiring nothing, knows not how to

301 1 Cor. ix. 19.
302 1 Tim. vi. 5.
303 Amos i. 13.
304 Cp. 2 Cor. vi. 11.
305 Matt. vi. 26.
306 Matt. vi. 25, 31.
307 2 Cor. vi. 10.

think about the morrow.[308] They exact from the poor that which they may give to the rich; Malachy implores the rich to provide for the poor. They empty the purses of their subjects; he for their sins *heaps altars* with vows and *peace-offerings*.[309] They build lofty palaces, raise up towers and ramparts to the heavens.[310] Malachy, *not having where to lay his head,*[311] *does the work of an evangelist*.[312] They *ride on horses*[313] with a crowd of men, who *eat bread for nought*, and that not *their own*;[314] Malachy, hedged round with a college of holy brothers, goes about on foot, bearing *the bread of angels*,[315] with which to *satisfy the hungry souls*.[316] They do not even know the congregations; he instructs them. They honour powerful men and tyrants; he punishes them. O, apostolic man, whom so many and so striking *signs of his apostleship*[317] ennoble! What wonder, then, if he has

308 Cp. Matt. vi. 34.
309 Exod. xxxii. 6, etc.
310 Cp. Gen. xi. 4.
311 Matt. viii. 20; Luke ix. 58.
312 2 Tim. iv. 5.
313 Jer. vi. 23, etc.
314 2 Thess. iii. 8, 12.
315 Ps. lxxviii. 25.
316 Ps. cvii. 9.
317 2 Cor. xii. 12 (vg.).

wrought wondrous things when he himself is so wonderful? Yet truly not he but God in him.[318] Moreover, it is said, *Thou art the God that doest wonders.*[319]

45. (25). There was a woman in the city of Coleraine who had a demon. Malachy was called; he prayed for the possessed; he commanded the invader and he went out. But his iniquity was not yet fully satisfied, and he entered into an unhappy woman who happened to be standing by. And Malachy said, "I did not release that woman from your grasp in order that you might enter this one; go out of her also." He obeyed, but went back to the former woman; and driven forth from her once more, he again went into the second. So for some time he vexed them alternately, fleeing to and fro. Then the saint, indignant that he was mocked by a demon, summoned up his spirit, and shouted; and when he had made an attack on the adversary with all the forces of faith, he drove the demon away from both, no less vexed than those whom he had vexed. But do not suppose, reader, that the delay which he caused the saint was due to his own strength: it was permitted by the divine dispensation, evidently in order that by this as

318 Cp. 1 Cor. xv. 10.

319 Ps. lxxvii. 14.

well the power of the evil one as the victory of Malachy might be made more manifest.

Hear now what he did elsewhere, but not by reason of his presence. Assuredly what he had power to accomplish when absent, he could do also when present.

46. In a district of the northern part of Ireland a sick man lay in his house. His sickness was beyond doubt due to the evil influence of demons. For one night he heard them talking; and one said to another, "See that this wretched man does not touch the bed or bedding of that hypocrite, and so escape from our hands." The man perceived that they were speaking of Malachy, who, as he remembered, had not long before passed a night in that house. And the bedding was still in its place; and taking courage, with his utmost effort he began to crawl, weak in body but strong in faith. And lo, in the air there was clamour and shouting: "Stop him, stop him, hold him, hold him; we are losing our prey." But, carried on by faith and the desire to escape, the more they shouted the more he hastened to the remedy, straining with knees and hands. And when he reached the couch, and went up on it, he rolled himself in the bed-clothes, and heard the wailing of them

that lamented, "Alas, alas, we have betrayed ourselves, we have been deceived, he has escaped." And quicker than a word, there left him the terror of the demons and the horror which he suffered, and with them all his sickness.

In the city of Lismore a man vexed by a demon was delivered by Malachy.

Also once, when he was passing through Leinster, an infant was brought to him who had a demon, and he was brought back whole.

In the same region he ordered a mad woman, bound with cords, to be loosed and to be bathed in water which he blessed. She washed and was healed.

Another woman also in Saul, a region of Ulaid, who was tearing her own limbs with her teeth, he cured by praying and touching her.

There was a madman, who predicted many things to come. His friends and neighbours brought him to the man of God, bound strongly with cords, because his very madness had made him strong to do hurt and exceeding terrible. Malachy prayed, and immediately the sick man was healed and released. This was done in a certain place, the name of which we omit because it has a very barbarous sound, as also have many others.

At another time in the above-mentioned city of Lismore, the parents of a dumb girl brought her to him in the midst of the street as he passed, asking him with much entreaty that he would deign to help her. Malachy stood and prayed; and he *touched her tongue* with his finger and *spat*[320] upon her mouth, and sent her away speaking.

47. (26). Going out of a certain church he met a man with his wife, and she could not speak. And when he was asked to have mercy on her, he stood in the gate, the people surrounding him; and he gave a blessing upon her, and bade her say the Lord's Prayer. She said it, and the people blessed the Lord.

In a city called Antrim a certain man lying on a bed, now deprived for twelve days of the use of his tongue, at the bidding of the saint, who visited him, recovered his speech and received the Eucharist; and so fortified

---

320 Mark vii. 33.

he breathed his last breath in *a good confession.*[321] O, *fruitful olive tree in the house of God*![322] O, *oil* of gladness,[323] giving both anointing and light! By the splendour of the miracle he gave light to those who were whole, by the graciousness of the favour he anointed the sick man, and obtained for him, soon about to die, the saving power of confession and communion.

One of the nobles came in to him, *having somewhat to say to him*;[324] and while they were speaking, *full of faith*[325] piously stole three rushes from the couch on which Malachy sat, and took them with him: and God wrought many things as a result of the pious theft, by that man's faith and the sanctity of the prelate.

By chance he had come to a city called Cloyne. And when he was sitting at table a nobleman of that city came in and humbly prayed him for his wife, who was pregnant, and had passed the appointed time of parturition, so that all wondered, and there was none who

321 1 Tim. vi. 13.
322 Ps. lii. 8 (vg.).
323 Ps. xlv. 7.
324 Luke vii. 40.
325 Acts vi. 5.

did not believe that her life was in danger. With him also Nehemiah, the bishop of that city, who was sitting next to him, made request to Malachy, and others also as many as were present reclining together. Then he said, "I pity her, for she is a good and modest woman." And offering the man a cup which he had blessed, he said, "Go, give her to drink, and know that when she has taken the draught of blessing[326] she will bring forth without delay, and without danger." It was done as he commanded, and that very night there followed that which he promised.

He was sitting in a plain with the count of Ulaid, dealing with certain matters, *and a great multitude*[327] was about them. There came a woman who had long been with child. She declared that contrary to all the laws of nature she had already been pregnant for fifteen months and twenty days. Malachy having pity for this new and unheard-of trouble, prayed, and the woman was delivered. Those who were present rejoiced and wondered. For all saw with what ease and rapidity she brought forth in the same place, and the sad portent of birth denied was changed to a happier marvel.

---

326 Cp. 1 Cor. x. 16.

327 Luke vi. 17.

48. (27). There happened in the same place an event with a similar miracle but a different issue. He saw a man who was reported to be consorting publicly with his brother's concubine; and he was a knight, a servant of the count. And publicly accosting the incestuous man he displayed himself to him as another John, saying, *It is not lawful for thee to have thy brother's* concubine.[328] But he, nevertheless, in his turn displaying himself to Malachy as another Herod, not only did not hearken to him, but even answered him haughtily, and before them all swore that he would never put her away. Then Malachy, much agitated, for he was vehemently zealous for righteousness, said, "Then God shall separate you from her against your will." Paying little heed the man went away at once in a rage. And meeting the woman not far from the crowd which was in the place, he treated her evilly and with violence, as though he wholly belonged to *Satan* to whom he had a little before been *delivered.*[329] Nor was the crime hidden. The damsel who accompanied the lady ran back to the house (for it was not far from the place), and, breathless, announced the wickedness that had taken place. At the word her brothers, who were at home, enraged

328 Mark vi. 18.

329 1 Cor. v. 5; 1 Tim. i. 20.

at the dishonour done to their sister, rushed thither with all haste and slew the enemy of virtue, *taken in the very* place and *act*[330] of crime, piercing him with many wounds. The assembly was not yet dismissed when, lo! his armour-bearer proclaimed what had happened. And all wondered that the sentence of Malachy had taken such speedy effect. When this word was heard all evil-doers (for there were many in the land) feared and, being terrified, purified themselves, *washing their hands in the blood of the ungodly.*[331]

49. (28). Dermot the count, who had now for a long time lain on his bed, he sprinkled with blessed water, and caused him to rise up without delay, and so strong that he mounted his horse on the spot, surpassing assuredly the hope of himself and of his friends—rebuking him severely at the same time because he was a bad man *serving his belly*[332] and his appetite immoderately.

In the town of Cashel a man came before him with his paralysed son, asking that he should be healed. And Malachy, praying briefly, said, "*Go thy way; thy son*

330 John viii. 4.

331 Ps. lviii. 10 (vg.).

332 Rom. xvi. 18.

shall be made whole."[333] He went, and on the morrow he returned with his son, who was nevertheless by no means whole. Then Malachy rose and standing over him prayed at greater length, and he was made whole. And turning to the father he said, "Offer him to God." The man assented, but did not keep his promise; and after some years his son, now a young man, relapsed into the same state, no doubt because of his father's disobedience and his violation of the pledge.

Another man came from a long distance, when Malachy was in the borders of Munster, bringing to him his son, who was entirely deprived of the use of his feet. When he inquired how this had happened to him, he said, "As I suspect, by the malignity of demons"; adding, "It was they, if I mistake not, who, when he was playing in a field, *caused a sleep to fall* upon him,[334] and when the child awoke he found himself so." Saying this, he poured forth his petition with tears, and earnestly sought help. Malachy pitying him prayed, bidding the sick boy in the meantime to sleep there upon the ground. He slept, and he arose whole. Because he

333 John iv. 50.

334 Gen. ii. 21.

had *come from far*[335] he kept him some time in his company, and he used to walk with him.

50. In the monastery of Bangor a certain poor man was maintained by the alms of the brothers; and he received a small sum every day, for performing some office in the mill. He had been lame for twelve years, creeping on the ground with his hands, and dragging his dead feet after him. Him Malachy found one day before his cell, sad and sorrowful, and asked him the cause. And he said, "You see how for a long time I am miserably troubled and *the hand of the Lord is upon me*;[336] and lo, to increase my distress, men who ought to have had pity, rather laugh at me and cast my wretchedness in my teeth." And when he heard him, moved with compassion, he *looked up to heaven*,[337] at the same time raising his hands. Having said a short prayer he entered his cell, and the other rose up. And standing upon his feet he wondered if it was true, suspecting that he was in a dream.[338] But he began to move with slow steps, for he did not altogether believe that he could walk.

335 Mark viii. 3.

336 Acts xiii. 11, etc.

337 Mark vii. 34.

338 Cp. Acts xii. 9.

At length, *as it were waking out of a deep sleep,*[339] he recognized the mercy of the Lord upon him; he walked firmly, and returned to the mill *leaping* and exulting *and praising God.* When those saw him who had before seen and *known him* they *were filled with wonder and amazement,*[340] *supposing it to be a spirit.*[341]

Malachy likewise healed a dropsical man by praying, who remained there in the monastery and was appointed shepherd.

51. A city of Ireland called Cork was without a bishop. They proceeded to an election; but the various parties did not agree, each, as is usual, wishing to appoint their own bishop, not God's. Malachy came to the place when he heard of the disagreement. Calling together the clergy and people he took pains to unite the hearts and desires of the opposing parties. And when they had been persuaded that the whole business ought to be entrusted to him, on whom in a very special manner lay *the care of* that as also of the other *churches*[342]

---

339 Gen. xlv. 26 (vg.).

340 Acts iii. 8-10.

341 Mark vi. 49.

342 2 Cor. xi. 28.

throughout Ireland, immediately he named to them, not any of the nobles of the land, but rather a certain poor man whom he knew to be holy and learned; *and he was a stranger.*[343] He was sought; and it was announced that he was lying in bed, and so weak that he could in no wise go out unless carried in the hands of those who ministered to him. "Let him rise," said Malachy; "in the name of the Lord I command it; obedience will save him." What was he to do? He wished to obey, but he thought himself unfitted; for though it should be possible for him to go, he dreaded to be a bishop. So with the will to be obedient twin enemies were contending, the load of weakness and the fear of the burden. But the first conquered, the hope of salvation being given him as an aid. Therefore he made the attempt, he moved, tested his power, discovered that he was stronger than usual. Faith increased along with power, and again faith made stronger gave in its turn increase of power. Now he was able to rise unassisted, now to walk somewhat better, now not even to perceive weariness in walking; at length, to come to Malachy without difficulty and quickly, unaided by man. He promoted him, and put him into the chair, with the

343 Luke xvii. 16, 18.

applause of clergy and people. This was done without question, because neither did they dare to oppose the will of Malachy in any way, seeing the sign which he had wrought; nor did he hesitate to obey, being made surer, by so evident a proof, of the will of God.

52. (29). A certain *woman was diseased with an issue of blood*;[344] and she was of noble birth and very dear to Malachy, though by reason of the nobility rather of her character than of her descent. When she was entirely failing, her strength no doubt being exhausted with her blood, and was now near the end, she sent to the man of God, in order that—the only thing that remained to be done—he might help her soul who should see her no more in the body. When Malachy heard it he was troubled, because she was a woman of virtue, and her life fruitful in work and example. And perceiving that he could not reach her in time he called Malchus, for he was young and active (he is that brother of Abbot Christian whom we mentioned above), and said, "Haste, take her these three apples on which I have invoked the name of the Lord; I am assured of this, that when she tastes these she *shall not taste of death* before

344 Matt. ix. 20.

she sees us,[345] though we shall follow somewhat more slowly." Malchus hastened as he was commanded, and when he came he went in to the dying woman, showing himself another servant of Elisha, except that his work was more efficacious.[346] He bade her take that which Malachy had blessed and sent to her, and to taste it if by any means she could. But she was so refreshed when she heard Malachy's name, that she was able to obey, and indicated by a nod (for she could not speak) that she wished to be raised up for a little while. She was raised up, she tasted; she was strengthened by what she tasted, she spoke, and gave thanks. *And the Lord caused a deep sleep to fall upon* her,[347] and she rested most sweetly in it, having long ceased to enjoy the benefit of sleep, or to partake of food. Meanwhile *her blood was staunched*[348] and awaking after a while she found herself whole,[349] but she was still weak from long fasting and loss of blood. If in any degree the cure was not complete, on the following day the wished-for presence and appearance of Malachy made it perfect.

---

345 Matt. xvi. 28; Mark ix. 1; Luke ix. 27.

346 See 2 Kings iv. 29 ff.

347 Gen. ii. 21.

348 Luke viii. 44.

349 Cp. Mark v. 29.

53. (30). A nobleman lived in the neighbourhood of the monastery of Bangor, whose wife was *sick nigh unto death*.[350] Malachy, being asked to *come down ere she died*,[351] to *anoint the sick* woman *with oil*,[352] came down and went in to her; and when she saw him she rejoiced greatly, animated by the hope of salvation. And when he was preparing to anoint her, it seemed to all that it ought rather to be postponed to the morning; for it was evening. Malachy assented, and when he had given a blessing over the sick woman, he went out with those who were with him. But shortly afterwards, suddenly *there was a cry made*,[353] lamentation and great wailing through the whole house, for it was reported that she had died. Malachy ran up when he heard the tumult, and his disciples followed him. And coming to the bed, when he had assured himself that she had breathed her last, he was greatly troubled in mind, blaming himself that she had died without the grace of the sacrament. And lifting up his hands to heaven he said, "*I beseech thee*, Lord, *I have done very foolishly*. I, even *I*,

---

350 Phil. ii. 27 (inexact quotation).

351 John iv. 49.

352 Cp. Mark vi. 13; Jas. v. 14.

353 Matt. xxv. 6.

have sinned,[354] who postponed, not she who desired it." Saying this he protested in the hearing of all that *he* would not *be comforted*,[355] that he would give *no rest to his spirit*,[356] unless he should be allowed to restore the grace which he had taken away. And standing over her, all night *he laboured in his groaning*; and, instead of the holy oil, flooding the dead woman with a great rain of *tears*,[357] he bestowed on her such a substitute for the unction as he could. Thus did he; but to his companions he said, "*Watch and pray.*"[358] So they in psalms, he in tears, passed a night of vigil. And when the morning came the Lord heard His saint, for the *Spirit* of the Lord was *making intercession for him*, who *maketh intercession for* the saints *with groanings that cannot be uttered.*[359] Why more? She who had been dead *opened her eyes*,[360] and, as those do who wake from a deep sleep, rubbing her forehead and temples with her hands, she rose upon the bed, and recognizing Malachy, devoutly

354 1 Chron. xxi. 8, 17.

355 Gen. xxxvii. 35.

356 2 Cor. ii. 13; cp. Jer. xlv. 3.

357 Ps. vi. 6 (vg.); Jer. xlv. 3.

358 Matt. xxvi. 41, etc.

359 Rom. viii. 26.

360 Acts ix. 40.

saluted him with bowed head. And mourning being *turned into joy*,[361] amazement took hold of all, both those who saw and those who heard. And Malachy also gave thanks and blessed the Lord. And he anointed her, nevertheless, knowing that in that sacrament *sins are forgiven*, and that *the prayer of faith saves the sick*.[362] After this he went away, and she recovered, and after living for some time in good health, *that the* glory *of God should be made manifest in her*,[363] she accomplished the penance which Malachy had enjoined upon her, and again *fell asleep*[364] in a *good confession*,[365] and passed to the Lord.

54. (3). There was also a woman whom *a spirit of* anger and *fury*[366] dominated to such an extent that not only her neighbours and relatives fled from her society, but even her own sons could scarcely endure to live with her. Shouting, rancour and *a mighty tempest*[367] wherever she was. Violent, fiery, hasty, terrible with tongue

---

361 John xvi. 20.
362 Jas. v. 15.
363 John ix. 3.
364 Acts vii. 60.
365 1 Tim. vi. 13.
366 Exod. xv. 8 (vg.).
367 Ps. l. 3 (vg.).

and hand, intolerable to all, and hated. Her sons, grieving both for her and for themselves, dragged her into the presence of Malachy, setting forth their lamentable complaint with tears. But the holy man, pitying both the sickness of the mother and the trouble of her sons, called her aside, and made urgent inquiry whether she had ever confessed her sins. She replied, "Never." "Confess," said he. She obeyed; and he enjoined penance on her when she made confession, and prayed over her that Almighty God might give her *the spirit of meekness*,[368] and in the name of the Lord Jesus bade her to be angry no more. Such meekness followed that it was plain to all that it was nothing else than a marvellous *change effected by the right hand of the Most High*.[369] It is said that she is still living today, and is so patient and gentle that, though she used to exasperate all, now she cannot be exasperated by any injuries or insults or afflictions. If it be allowed me, as the Apostle says, *to be fully persuaded in my own mind*,[370] let each accept it as he will; for me, I give it as my opinion that this miracle should be regarded as superior to that of raising the dead woman, mentioned above, inasmuch as there the

368 1 Cor. iv. 21.

369 Ps. lxxvii. 10 (vg.).

370 Rom. xiv. 5.

outward, but here the *inner man*[371] was restored to life. And now let us hasten to what remains.

55. A man who as regards the world was honourable, as regards God devout, came to Malachy and complained to him concerning *the barrenness of his soul*,[372] praying that he would obtain for him from Almighty God the grace of tears. And Malachy, smiling because he was pleased that there should be spiritual desire from a man of the world, laid his cheek on the cheek of the other as though caressing him, and said, "*Be it done unto you as you have asked*."[373] From that time *rivers of waters ran down his eyes*[374] so great and so nearly incessant that the phrase of Scripture might seem applicable to him: "*A fountain of gardens, a well of living waters*."[375]

There is an island of the sea in Ireland, from of old fruitful of fishes; and the sea there abounds in fish. By the sins of the inhabitants, as it is believed, the wonted supply was taken away, and *she that had many*

371 Eph. iii. 16; cp. 2 Cor. iv. 16.

372 Ps. xxxv. 12 (vg.).

373 Matt. viii. 13, combined with John xv. 7.

374 Ps. cxix. 136.

375 Cant. iv. 15.

children was waxed feeble,[376] and her own great usefulness utterly dwindled away. While the natives were grieving, and the peoples taking ill the great loss, it was revealed to a certain woman that a remedy might be effected by the prayers of Malachy; and that became known to all, for she herself proclaimed it. By the will of God it happened that Malachy arrived. For while he was going round and filling the region with the Gospel, he turned aside thither that to them also he might impart the same grace.[377] But *the barbarous people*,[378] who cared more for the fishes,[379] demanded with all vehemence that he would deign to regard rather the sterility of their island. And when he answered that it was not for that he had come, but that he desired to catch men rather than fish,[380] yet seeing their faith[381] he *kneeled down on the shore and prayed*[382] to the Lord that, though they were unworthy of it, he would not deny them the benefit granted long before, since they sought

376 1 Sam. ii. 5.
377 Cp. Rom. i. 11.
378 Acts xxviii. 2.
379 Cp. 1 Cor. ix. 9.
380 Cp. Luke v. 10.
381 Cp. Mark ii. 5; Luke v. 20.
382 Acts xxi. 5.

it again with so great faith. *The prayer went up*,[383] there came up also *a multitude of fishes*,[384] and perhaps more fruitful than in ancient days; and the people of the land continue to enjoy that abundance to this day. What wonder if *the prayer of a righteous man* which *penetrates the heavens*,[385] penetrated *the abysses*,[386] and called forth from the depth of the sea so great supplies of fish?

56. There came, on one occasion, three bishops into the village of Faughart, which they say was the birthplace of Brigit the virgin; and Malachy was a fourth. And the presbyter who had received them with hospitality, said to him, "What shall I do, for I have no fish?" And when he answered that he should seek them from the fishermen, he said, "For the last two years no fish have been found in the river; and for that reason the fishermen also are all scattered and have even abandoned their art." And Malachy replied "Command them to *let down the nets*[387] in the name of the Lord." It was done, and twelve salmon were caught. They lowered

383 Acts x. 4.

384 Luke v. 6; John xxi. 6.

385 Ecclus. xxxv. 21 (inexact quotation).

386 Cp. Ps. cvii. 26 (vg.).

387 Luke v. 4.

them a second time, and catching as many more they brought to the tables both an unlooked-for dish and an unlooked-for miracle. And that it might be clear that this was granted to the merits of Malachy, the same sterility nevertheless continued also for the following two years.

Chapter VII

He does battle for the faith; he restores peace among those who were at variance; he takes in hand to build a stone church.

57. (32). There was a certain clerk in Lismore whose life, as it is said, was good, but his faith not so. He was a man of some knowledge in his own eyes, and dared to say that in the Eucharist there is only a sacrament and not the fact of the sacrament, that is, mere sanctification and not the truth of the Body. On this subject he was often addressed by Malachy in secret, but in vain; and finally he was called before a public assembly, the laity however being excluded, in order that if it were possible, he should be healed and not put to confusion. So in a gathering of clerics the man was given opportunity to answer for his opinion. And when with all his powers of ingenuity, in which he had no slight skill, he attempted to assert and defend his error, Malachy disputing against him and convicting him, in the judgement of all, he was worsted; and he

retired, put to confusion by the unanimity though not sentenced to punishment. But he said that he was not overcome by reason, but crushed by the authority of the bishop. "And you, Malachy," said he, "have put me to confusion this day without good reason, speaking assuredly against the truth and contrary to your own conscience." Malachy, sad for a man so hardened, but grieving more for the injury that was done to the faith, and fearing dangerous developments, called the church together, publicly censured the erring one, publicly admonished him to repent, the bishops and the whole clergy urging him to the same effect. When he did not submit, they pronounced an anathema upon him as contumacious and proclaimed him a heretic. But not aroused from sleep by this he said, "You all favour the man, not the truth; I do not accept persons so that I should *forsake the truth*."[388] To this word the saint made answer with some heat, "The Lord make you confess the truth even of necessity;" and when he replied "Amen" the assembly was dissolved. Burnt with such a branding-iron he meditated flight, for he could not bear to be of ill repute and dishonoured. And forthwith he departed, carrying his belongings; when lo, seized

388 Prov. xxviii. 21 (vg.).

with sudden weakness, he stood still, and his strength failing he threw himself on the ground in the same spot, panting and weary. A vagabond madman, arriving by chance at that place, came upon the man and asked him what he did there. He replied that he was suffering from great weakness and unable either to advance or to go back. And the other said, "This weakness is nothing else than death itself." *But this he spake not of himself, but*[389] God fitly rebuked by means of a madman him who would not submit to the sane counsels of men of understanding. And he said, "Return home, I will help you." Finally with his guidance he went back into the city: he returned to his right mind and to the mercy of the Lord. In the same hour the bishop was summoned, the truth was acknowledged, error was renounced. He confessed his guilt and was absolved. He asked for the viaticum, and reconciliation was granted; and almost in the same moment his perfidy was renounced by his mouth and dissolved by his death. So, to the wonder of all, with all speed was fulfilled the word of Malachy, and with it that of the Scripture which says, "*Trouble gives understanding to the hearing.*"[390]

389 John xi. 51.

390 Isa. xxviii. 19 (vg.).

58. (33). Between the peoples of certain regions there once arose grievous discord. Malachy was importuned to make peace between them, and because he was hindered by other business he committed this matter to one of the bishops. He made excuse and refused, saying that Malachy, not he, had been sought for, that he would be despised, that he was unwilling to take trouble to no purpose. "*Go*," said Malachy, "*and the Lord be with you*."[391] He replied, "I assent, but if they will not hear me, know that I will appeal to your Fatherhood." Smiling, Malachy said, "Be it so." Then the bishop, having called the parties together, dictated terms of peace; they assented and were reconciled to one another, security was given on both sides, and peace was established; and so he dismissed them. But one party, seeing that their enemies had become careless and were unprepared, because peace having been made they suspected no harm, *said* among themselves, each man *to his neighbour*,[392] "What are we minded to do? Victory and vengeance on our foes is in our grasp"; and they began to attack them. What was happening became known to the bishop, and hastening up he charged their chief with wickedness and guile, but he

391 1 Sam. xvii. 37, combined with 1 Chron. xxii. 16.

392 Gen. xi. 3 (vg.).

treated him with contempt. He invoked the name of Malachy against him, and he paid no attention to it. Laughing at the bishop he said, "Do you suppose that for you we ought to let those go who did evil to us, whom *God hath delivered into our hands*?"[393] And the bishop, remembering the conversation which he had had with Malachy, *weeping and wailing*,[394] turned his face towards Malachy's monastery and said, "Where art thou, man of God, where art thou? Is not this, my father, what I told thee of? Alas, alas, I came here that I might do good and not evil; and behold, through me all are perishing, these in the body, those in the soul." Many things in this manner said he as he *mourned* and *lamented*,[395] and he urged and addressed Malachy, as though he were present, against the wicked. But meanwhile the impious men did not cease to attack those with whom they had made peace, so as to destroy them; and behold there was *a lying spirit in the mouth of* certain men to *deceive* them.[396] And these men met them in the way announcing that a raid had been made into their lands by their adversaries, that all things were

---

393 Judg. xvi. 24.

394 Mark v. 38.

395 Matt. xi. 17.

396 1 Kings xxii. 22; 2 Chron. xviii. 21.

being consumed *with the edge of the sword*,[397] and that their goods were being laid waste, and their wives and children taken and led away. When they heard this they returned in haste. The hindmost followed the first, *not knowing whither they went*[398] or what had happened; for they had not all heard the men who spoke. And when they came and found none of those things which had been told them they were confounded, taken in their own wickedness;[399] and they *knew* that they had been given up to *the spirit of error*,[400] on account of the messenger of Malachy whom they deceived and his *name* which *they despised*.[401] Further, the bishop, when he heard that the traitors were foiled in the iniquity which they had devised, returned with joy to Malachy and told him all things in order which had happened to him.

59. Malachy, knowing that by such an event the peace was disturbed, taking suitable opportunity was at pains in his own person to restore peace once more between

397 Josh. vi. 21; Judg. iv. 15, etc.
398 Heb. xi. 8.
399 Cp. Ps. x. 2.
400 1 John iv. 6.
401 Cp. Mal. i. 6.

them, and to confirm it when restored by the giving and receiving of security and an oath on both sides. But those who before had suffered from the violation of peace, mindful of the injury, and ignoring the agreement and the command of Malachy, took in hand to make reprisals. And all coming together, they set out to take their enemies unprepared and to return upon their own head the evil which they had thought to do to them.[402] And when they had very easily forded a great river which lay between them, they were stopped by a rivulet to which they came, not far from it. For indeed now it was not a rivulet, but appeared clearly to be a huge river, denying passage in every part of it to those who desired to cross it. All wondered that it was now so great, knowing how small it had been before, and they said among themselves, "What has caused this inundation? The air is clear, there are no rains, and we do not remember that there have been any lately; and even if there had been much rain, which of us remembers that, to however great a flood it swelled, it ever before covered the land, spreading over sown ground and meadow? *This is the finger of God*,[403] and the Lord

402 Cp. Ps. vii. 16.

403 Exod. viii. 19.

is hedging up our ways,[404] on account of Malachy, His saint, whose *covenant we have transgressed*[405] and disobeyed his commandment." So these also, without accomplishing their purpose, returned to their own territory, likewise confounded. The report was spread *throughout all the region;*[406] and they blessed God, who *took the wise in their own craftiness,*[407] *and cutting off the horns of the wicked,*[408] *exalted the horn of His anointed.*[409]

60. One of the nobles hostile to the king was reconciled by means of Malachy. For he did not trust the king sufficiently to make peace with him except by the mediation of Malachy, or of one for whom the king had equal reverence. His distrust was not unfounded, as afterwards appeared. For when he had become careless, and was no longer taking precautions, the king captured him and put him in bonds, more truly himself captured by ancient hate. His own friends demanded him by *the hand of the mediator;*[410] for neither did they

404 Hos. ii. 6.
405 Josh. vii. 15, etc.
406 Cp. Luke iv. 14, etc.
407 Job v. 13, combined with 1 Cor. iii. 19.
408 Ps. lxxv. 10.
409 1 Sam. ii. 10.
410 Gal iii. 19.

expect anything but his death. What should Malachy do? There was nothing to be done except to recur to that one accustomed refuge of his. Gathering an exceeding mighty army, a great crowd of his own disciples, he went to the king, and demanded him who was bound; he was refused. But Malachy said, "You act unrighteously against the Lord, and against me, and against yourself, *transgressing the covenant*;[411] if you disregard it, yet shall not I. A man has entrusted himself to my guarantee; if he should die, I have betrayed him. I am guilty of his blood. Why has it seemed good to you to make me a traitor, yourself a transgressor? Know that *I will eat nothing until*[412] he is liberated; no, nor these either." Having said this he entered the church. He called upon Almighty God with anxious groanings, his own and those of his disciples, that He would deign to *deliver out of the hand of the transgressor and cruel man*[413] him who was unjustly sentenced. And that day and the following night they persisted in fasting and prayer. Word was brought to the king of that which was being done; and his *heart was* the more *hardened*[414] by that

411 Josh. vii. 15, etc.

412 Acts xxiii. 14.

413 Ps. lxxi. 4 (inexact quotation).

414 Exod. viii. 19.

by which it ought to have been softened. The carnal man took to flight, fearing lest if he remained near at hand he might not be able to withstand the power of prayer; as though, forsooth, if he was hidden it could not find him, nor would penetrate to a remote place. Do you put bounds, wretched man, to *the prayers of saints*?[415] Is prayer an arrow that has been shot, that you may *flee from the face of the bow*?[416] *Whither wilt thou go from the Spirit of God*, who carries it, *or whither wilt thou flee from His presence*?[417] At last Malachy pursues the fugitive, he finds him who lies hidden. "*You shall be blind and not seeing*,[418] that you may see better, and may understand that *it is hard for you to kick against the pricks.*[419] Nay, perceive even now that *sharp arrows of the mighty*[420] have come to you, which, although they have rebounded from your heart, because it is of stone, have not rebounded from your eyes. Would that even through the windows of the eyes they might reach to

---

415 Rev. v. 8.
416 Isa. xxi. 15 (vg.).
417 Ps. cxxxix. 7.
418 Acts xiii. 11.
419 Acts xxvi. 14.
420 Ps. cxx. 4.

the heart, and *trouble give understanding*[421] to blindness." It could be seen that *Saul* again was *led by the hand*[422] and brought to Ananias, a wolf to a sheep, that he might disgorge his prey. He disgorged it and *received sight*,[423] for to such a degree was Malachy like a sheep, if, for example, it were to take pity even on the wolf. Note carefully from this, reader, with whom Malachy had his dwelling, what sort of princes they were, what sort of peoples. How is it that he also was not *a brother to dragons, and a companion to owls*?[424] And therefore the Lord *gave him power to tread upon serpents and scorpions*,[425] *to bind their kings with chains and their nobles with fetters of iron*.[426] Hear now what follows.

61. (34). He to whom Malachy had yielded the possessions of the monastery of Bangor, ungrateful for the benefit, from that time forward behaved himself always most arrogantly against him and his followers, hostile to them in all things, plotting everywhere, and

---

421 Isa. xxviii. 19.

422 Acts ix. 8.

423 Acts ix. 18.

424 Job xxx. 29.

425 Luke x. 19 (quotation not exact).

426 Ps. cxlix.

disparaging his deeds. But not without punishment. He had an only son, who, imitating his father and daring himself to act in opposition to Malachy, died the same year. And thus he died. It seemed good to Malachy that a stone oratory should be erected at Bangor like those which he had seen constructed in other regions. And when he began to lay the foundations the natives wondered, because in that land no such buildings were yet to be found. But that worthless fellow, presumptuous and arrogant as he was, not only wondered but was indignant. And from that indignation *he conceived grief and brought forth iniquity*.[427] And he became a *talebearer among the peoples*,[428] now *disparaging secretly*,[429] now speaking evil openly; drawing attention to Malachy's frivolity, shuddering at the novelty, exaggerating the expense. With such poisonous words as these he was urging and inducing many to put a stop to it: "Follow me, and what ought not to be done by any but ourselves let us not permit to be done against our will." Then with many whom he was able to persuade—*himself the* first *leader in speech*[430] as well as the origin of the

427 Job xv. 35 (vg.); Ps. vii. 14 (vg.).

428 Lev. xix. 16.

429 Ps. ci. 5.

430 Acts xiv. 12.

evil—he went down to the place, and finding the man of God accosted him: "Good sir, why have you thought good to introduce this novelty into our regions? We are Scots, not Gauls. What is this frivolity? What need was there for a work so superfluous, so proud? Where will you, *a poor and needy man*,[431] find *the means to finish it*?[432] Who will see it finished? What sort of presumption is this, to begin, I say not what you cannot finish, but what you cannot even see finished? Though indeed it is the act of a maniac rather than of a presumptuous man to attempt what is beyond his measure, what exceeds his strength, what baffles his abilities. Cease, cease, desist from this madness. If not, we shall not permit it, we shall not tolerate it." This he said, proclaiming what he would do, but not considering what it was within his power to do. For some of those on whom he counted and whom he had brought with him, when they saw the man changed their minds and went no more with him.[433]

62. And to him the holy man spoke quite freely: "Wretched man, the work which you see begun, and on

431 Ps. lxxiv. 21.

432 Luke xiv. 28.

433 Cp. John vi. 66.

which you look askance, shall undoubtedly be finished: many shall see it finished. But you, because you do not wish it, will not see it; and that which you wish not shall be yours—to die: take heed that you do not *die in your sins*."[434] So it happened: he died, and the work was finished; but he saw it not, for, as we have said already, he died the same year. Meanwhile the father, who soon heard what the holy man had foretold concerning his son, and knew that his word was *quick and powerful*,[435] said, "He *has slain my son*."[436] And by the instigation of the devil he burned with such rage against him that he was not afraid, before the duke and magnates of Ulaid, to accuse of falsehood and lying him who was most truthful and a disciple and lover of the Truth; and he used violent language against him, calling him an ape. And Malachy, who had been taught not to *render railing for railing*,[437] *was dumb, and opened not his mouth*[438] *while the wicked was before him*.[439] But the Lord was not forgetful of His word which He had spoken, *Ven-*

434 John viii. 21.

435 Heb. iv. 12.

436 1 Kings xvii. 18.

437 1 Pet. iii. 9.

438 Isa. liii. 7.

439 Ps. xxxix. 1.

geance is mine, I will repay.[440] The same day when the man returned home he expiated the rashness of his unbridled tongue, the avenger being the very one at whose instigation he had let it loose. The demon seized him and cast him into the fire, but he was soon pulled out by those that stood by; yet with his body partly burnt, and deprived of reason. And while he was raving Malachy was called, and when he came he found the accursed man, his foaming mouth contorted, terrifying all things with horrible sounds and movements, his whole body writhing, and scarcely to be kept in restraint by many men. And when he prayed for his enemy the man of all perfection was heard, but only in part. For in a moment, while the saint was praying, he opened his eyes, and recovered his understanding. But *an evil spirit of the Lord*[441] was left to him *to buffet him,*[442] *that he might learn not to blaspheme.*[443] We believe that he still lives, and up to this time is expiating the great sin which he sinned against the saint; but they say that at certain times he is a lunatic. Further, the aforesaid possessions, since he could no longer hold them by reason

---

440 Rom. xii. 19.

441 1 Sam. xvi. 14; xix. 9 (vg.).

442 2 Cor. xii. 7

443 1 Tim. i. 20.

of his helplessness and uselessness, returned in peace to the place to which they had belonged. Nor did Malachy refuse them, when the prospect of peace was held out at length after so much trouble.

63. But now our narrative must return to the work of the building which Malachy had undertaken. And though Malachy had not the means, I do not say to finish it, but to do any part of it, yet *his heart trusted in the Lord.*[444] The Lord, in fact, provided that, though he *set not his hope on treasures of money,*[445] money should not be lacking. For who else caused a treasure to be stored in that place, and being stored, not to be found till the time and work of Malachy? The servant of God found in God's purse what was not in his own. Deservedly, indeed. For what more just than that he who for God's sake possessed nothing should enter into partnership with God, and that they should both *have one purse.*[446] For the man who believes, the whole world is a treasury of riches; and what is it but a kind of purse of God? Indeed He says, *The world is mine, and the*

444 Dan. xiii. 35.

445 Ecclus. xxxi. 8 (vg.: with variant).

446 Prov. i. 14.

fulness thereof.[447] Hence it was that when many pieces of silver were found Malachy did not put them back in their place, but took them out of their place; for he bade the whole gift of God to be spent on the work of God. He considered not his own necessities nor those of his companions, but *cast his* thought upon *the Lord,*[448] to whom he did not doubt that he ought to resort as often as need required. And there is no doubt that that was the work of God, because Malachy had foreseen it by God's revelation. He had first consulted with the brothers concerning that work; and many on account of their lack of means were unwilling to assent to it. Anxious therefore and doubtful what he should do, he began to inquire earnestly in prayer what was the will of God. And one day coming back from a journey, when he drew near to the place he viewed it some way off; and lo, there appeared a great oratory, of stone and very beautiful. And paying careful attention to its position, form and construction, he took up the work with confidence, having first however related the vision to a few of the elder brothers. Indeed so carefully did he adhere to all his attentive observations regarding place and manner and quality that when the work was fin-

447 Ps. l. 12.

448 Ps. lv. 23 (vg.).

ished that which was made appeared closely similar to that which he had seen, as if he also as well as Moses had heard the saying, *Look* that *thou make all things according to the pattern shewed to thee in the mount.*[449] By the same kind of vision there was shown to him before it was built, not only the oratory, but also the whole monastery, which is situated at Saul.

64. (35). As he was passing through a certain city and a great multitude was running together to him, by chance he saw a young man among the rest eager *to see* him. He had *climbed up* on a stone, and standing on tip-toes, with outstretched neck, contemplating him with eyes and mind, showed himself to him as a kind of new Zacchaeus.[450] And it was not hid from Malachy (for the Holy Spirit revealed it) that he had truly come *in the spirit and power of* Zacchaeus.[451] He took no notice, however, at the time, and passed on in silence. But in the hospice that night he told the brothers how he had seen him and what he had foreseen concerning him. But on the third day behold he came with a certain nobleman, his lord, who disclosed

---

449 Heb. viii. 5.

450 Luke xix. 1-4.

451 Luke i. 17.

the wish and desire of the young man, and asked that he would deign to receive him on his commendation, and have him henceforth among his companions. And Malachy recognizing him said, "There is no need that man should commend him *whom* already *God has commended*."[452] And taking him by the hand he delivered him over to our abbot Congan and he to the brothers. But that young man—still living if I mistake not—the first lay conversus of the monastery of the Suir, has testimony from all that he lives a holy life among the brothers, according to the Cistercian Order. And the disciples recognized also in this incident that Malachy had *the spirit of prophecy*,[453] and not in this only, but in that which we shall add.

65. When he was offering the sacraments, and the deacon had approached him to do something belonging to his office, the priest beholding him groaned because he had perceived that something was hidden in him that was not meet. When the sacrifice was over, having been probed privately concerning his conscience *he confessed*

452 2 Cor. x. 18.

453 Rev. xix. 10.

and denied not[454] that he had been *mocked*[455] in a dream that night. And Malachy enjoined penance upon him and said, "It was your duty not to have ministered today, but reverently to withdraw from sacred things and to show respect to so great and divine mysteries, that purified by this humiliation you might in future minister more worthily."

Likewise on another occasion, when he was sacrificing and praying at the hour of sacrifice with his accustomed sanctity and purity of heart, the deacon standing by him, a dove was seen to enter through the window in great glory. And with that glory the priest was completely flooded, and the whole of the gloomy basilica became suffused with light. But the dove, after flitting about for a while, at length settled down on the cross before the face of the priest. The deacon was amazed; and trembling on account of the novelty both of the light and of the bird, for that is a rare bird in the land, fell upon his face, and palpitating, scarcely dared to rise even when the necessity of his office required it. After Mass Malachy spoke to him privately and bade him, as

454 John i. 20.

455 Gen. xxxix. 17.

he valued his life, on no account to divulge the mystery which he had seen, as long as he himself was alive.

Once, when he was at Armagh with one of his fellow-bishops, he rose in the night and began to go round the memorials of the saints, of which there are many in the cemetery of St. Patrick, with prayer. And lo, they saw one of the altars suddenly take fire. For both saw this great vision, and both wondered. And Malachy, understanding that it was a sign of the great merit of him, or those, whose bodies rested under that altar, ran and plunged into the midst of the flames with outstretched arms and embraced the sacred altar. What he did there, or what he perceived, none knows; but that from that fire he went forth ablaze more than his wont with heavenly fire, I suppose there is none of the brothers who were with him then that does not know.

66. These things have been mentioned, a few out of many, but many for this time. For these are not times of signs, as it is written, *We see not signs; there is no more any prophet.*[456] Whence it appears sufficiently how great in merits was my Malachy, who was so rich in signs, rare as they now are. For in what kind of *ancient*

456 Ps. lxxiv. 9.

miracles was not Malachy conspicuous? If we consider well those few that have been mentioned, he lacked not prophecy, nor revelation, nor vengeance upon the impious, nor *the grace of healings*,[457] nor transformation of minds, nor lastly raising the dead. By all these things God was blessed who so loved and adorned him, who also magnified him *before kings*,[458] and gave him *the crown of glory*.[459] That he was loved is proved in his merits, that he was adorned, in his signs, that he was magnified, in his vengeance on enemies, that he had glory, in recompense of rewards. You have in Malachy, diligent reader, something to wonder at, you have also something to imitate. Now carefully note what you may hope for as the result of these things. For *the end of these things is a precious death*.[460]

---

457 1 Cor. xii. 9 (vg.).

458 Ps. cxix. 46.

459 1 Pet. v. 4.

460 Rom. vi. 21, combined with Ps. cxvi. 15.

Chapter VIII

Departure from Ireland. Death and Burial at Clairvaux.

67. (30). Being asked once, in what place, if a choice were given him, he would prefer to spend his last day—for on this subject the brothers used to ask one another what place each would select for himself—he hesitated, and made no reply. But when they insisted, he said, "If I take my departure hence I shall do so nowhere more gladly than whence I may rise together with our Apostle"—he referred to St. Patrick; "but if it behoves me to make a pilgrimage, and if God so permits, I have selected Clairvaux." When asked also about the time, [he named in reply] the festival of all the dead. If it is regarded as a mere wish, it was fulfilled, if as a prophecy, not *a jot passed* from it.[461] *As we have heard so have we seen*[462] alike concerning place and day. Let us relate briefly in what order and by what occasion it

461 Matt. v. 18.

462 Ps. xlviii. 8.

came to pass. Malachy took it amiss that Ireland was still without a pall; for he was zealous for the sacraments, and would not that his nation should be wholly deprived of any one of them. And remembering that it had been promised to him by Pope Innocent, he was the more sad that while he was still alive it had not been sent for. And taking advantage of the fact that Pope Eugenius held the chief rule and was reported to have gone at that time to France, he rejoiced that he had found opportunity for claiming it. He took for granted that, the Pope being such a man as he was, and having been promoted from such a religious profession—and the more because he had been a special son of his own Clairvaux—he need not fear that he should have any difficulty with him. Therefore the bishops were summoned; a council assembled. Matters which were of immediate importance at the time were discussed for three days, and on the fourth the scheme of obtaining the pall was broached. Assent was given, but on condition that it should be obtained by another. However, since the journey was a comparatively short one, and on that account the pilgrimage seemed more easy to be endured, none presumed to oppose his counsel and will. And when the council was dissolved Malachy started on his way. Such brothers as had come together followed him to the shore; but not many, for he doubtless restrained them. One of them, Catholicus by name, with tearful voice and face, said to him, "Alas! you are going away; and in how great, almost daily, trouble you leave me you are not ignorant, and yet you do not, of your pity, give me help. If I deserve to suffer, what sin have the brothers committed that they are scarcely allowed to have any day or night free from the labour of caring for and guarding me?" By these words and tears of his son (for he wept) the father's *heart was* troubled,[463] and he embraced him with caresses, and making the sign of the cross on his breast said, "Be assured that you will have no such suffering till I return." Now he was an epileptic, and fell often; insomuch that at times he suffered not once but many times a day. He had been a victim to this horrible disease for six years; but at the word of Malachy he made a perfect recovery. From that hour he has suffered no such thing; no such thing, as we believe, will he suffer henceforth, for henceforth Malachy will not return.

68. When he was just about to embark there *came unto him* two of those who *clave unto him*[464] more closely,

---

463 Cp. Lam. ii. 11.

464 Ruth i. 14.

boldly *desiring a certain thing of him*. And he said to them, *"What would ye?"*[465] And they answered, "We will not say, except you promise that you will give it." He pledged himself. And they said, "We would have you certainly promise of your condescension, that you will return in good health to Ireland." All the others also insisted upon it. Then he deliberated for a while, repenting at first that he had bound himself, and not finding any way of escape. He was *straitened on every side*,[466] while no way of safety presented itself from both dangers—of forfeiting his wish and of breaking his promise. It seemed at length that he should rather choose that which influenced him more strongly at the moment, and leave the rest to higher guidance. He assented, sadly it is true; but he was more unwilling that they should be made sad; and pledging himself as they wished, he went on board the ship. And when they had completed nearly half the voyage suddenly a contrary wind drove the ship back and brought it to the land of Ireland again. Leaving the ship he passed the night in the port itself in one of his churches. And he joyfully gave thanks for the resourcefulness of the divine providence, by which it came about that he had

465 Matt. xx. 20, combined with Mark x. 35, 36.

466 Dan. xiii. 22.

now satisfied his promise. But in the morning, he went on board, and the same day, after a prosperous crossing, came into Scotland. On the third day he reached a place which is called Viride Stagnum; which he had caused to be prepared that he might found an abbey there. And leaving there some of his sons, our brothers, as a convent of monks and abbot (for he had brought them with him for that purpose) he bade them farewell and set out.

69. And as he passed on, King David met him, by whom he was received with joy and was detained as his guest for some days. And having done many things pleasing to God he resumed the journey that he had begun. And passing through Scotland, at the very border of England he went aside to the Church of Gisburn, where there dwell religious men leading a canonical life, familiar to him of old for their religious conversation and honourable character. At that place a woman was brought to him, suffering from a disease horrible to see, which is commonly called cancer; and he healed her. For when water which he blessed was sprinkled on the sores she ceased to feel pain. On the next day scarcely a sore was to be seen.

Departing thence he came to the sea, but was refused passage. The reason, if I am not mistaken, was that some difference had arisen between the chief pontiff and the king of England: for the king suspected in that good man I know not what evil, if he should cross the sea; for neither did he allow other bishops to cross. That obstacle, though contrary to the will of Malachy, was not contrary to the object of his wish. He grieved that the attainment of his desire should be postponed, not knowing that by this it would be the rather fulfilled. For if he had immediately passed over the sea he would have been obliged to pass by Clairvaux in order to follow the chief Pontiff. For by that time he had left it and was at or near Rome. But now through this delay it was brought about that he crossed later, and so, as was fitting, he came to the place of his most holy death, and at the hour of its approach.

70. (37). And he was received by us, though he came from the west, as the true *day-spring from on high visiting us.*[467] O, how greatly did that radiant sun fill our Clairvaux with added glory! How pleasant was the festal day that dawned upon us at his coming! *This was*

467 Luke i. 78.

the day which the Lord had made, we rejoiced and were glad in it.[468] As for me, with what rapid and bounding step, though trembling and weak, did I soon *run* to meet him! With what joy I *kissed him*! With what joyful arms I *embraced*[469] this grace sent to me from heaven! With what eager face and mind, my father, *I brought thee into my mother's house and into the chamber of her that conceived me*![470] What festive days I spent with thee then, though few! But how did he in his turn greet us? In truth our pilgrim showed himself cheerful and kindly to all, to all incredibly gracious. *How good and how pleasant*[471] a part he played among us as our guest; whom, forsooth, *he had come from the uttermost parts of the earth* to see, not that he should *hear*, but that he should show us, a *Solomon*! In fact we *heard* his *wisdom*,[472] we had his presence, and we have it still. Already four or five days of this our festival had passed, when lo, on the feast day of Blessed Luke the Evangelist, when he had celebrated Mass in the convent with that holy devotion of his, he was taken with a fever and

468 Ps. cxviii. 24.

469 Gen. xxix. 13.

470 Cant. iii. 4.

471 Ps. cxxxiii. 1.

472 Matt. xii. 42; Luke xi. 31.

lay down in his bed: and all of us were [sick] with him. *The end of our mirth is sorrow*,[473] but moderate sorrow, because for a time the fever seemed to be slight. You should see the brothers running about, eager to give, or to receive. To whom was it not sweet to see him? To whom was it not sweeter to minister to him? Both were pleasant and both salutary. It was an act of kindness to do him service, and it was repaid also to each one of them, by the gift of grace. All assisted, all were busied *with much serving*,[474] searching for medicines, applying poultices, urging him often to eat. But he said to them, "These things are without avail, yet for love of you I do whatever you bid me." For he knew that *the time* of his departure was at hand.[475]

71. And when the brothers who had come with him urged him more boldly, saying that it behoved him not to despair of life, for that no signs of death appeared in him, he said, "It behoves Malachy to leave the body this year." And he added, "See, the day is drawing near which, as you very well know, I have always desired

473 Prov. xiv. 13 (inexact quotation).

474 Luke x. 40.

475 Cp. 2 Tim. iv. 6.

to be the day of *my dissolution.*[476] *I know whom I have believed and am persuaded*;[477] I shall *not be disappointed of* the rest of *my desire*,[478] since I already have part of it. He who by his mercy has led me to the place which I sought, will not deny me the time for which I wished no less. As regards this mean body, *here is my rest*;[479] as regards my soul, the Lord will provide, *who saveth them that put their trust in Him.*[480] And *there is* no small hope *laid up for me at that day*[481] in which so great benefits are bestowed by the living on the dead." Not far away was that day when he spoke thus. Meanwhile he ordered that he should be anointed with the sacred oil. When the convent of brothers was going out that it might be done solemnly, he would not permit them to come up to him; he went down to them. For he was lying in the balcony of the upper house. He was anointed; and when he had received the viaticum, he commended himself to the prayers of the brothers, and the brothers to God, and went back to bed. He went down from the

476 2 Tim. iv. 6.

477 2 Tim. i. 12.

478 Ps. lxxviii. 30 (vg.).

479 Ps. cxxxii. 14 (inexact quotation).

480 Ps. xvii. 7.

481 2 Tim. iv. 8.

high balcony on his feet, and again, as if that were not enough, he went up on his feet; yet he said that death *was at the doors.*[482] Who should believe that this man was dying? Himself alone and God could know it. His face did not seem to have become pallid or wasted. His brow was not wrinkled, his eyes were not sunken, his nostrils were not thin, his lips were not contracted, his teeth were not brown, his neck was not gaunt and lean, his shoulders were not bowed, the flesh on the rest of his body had not failed. Such was the grace of his body, and such the *glory of his countenance which was* not *to be done away*,[483] even in death. As he appeared in life so was he also in death, more like to one alive.

72. (38). Hitherto our story has run a rapid course; but now it stays because Malachy *has finished his course.*[484] He is still, and with him we are still. Moreover, who would willingly hasten to [tell of] death? Especially thy death, holy father, who could describe it? Who would wish to hear the story? Yet we loved *in life, in death we shall not be divided.*[485] Brothers, let us not forsake in

---

482 Matt. xxiv. 33.

483 2 Cor. iii. 7.

484 Tim. iv. 7.

485 2 Sam. i. 23 (inaccurate quotation).

death him with whom we companied in life. From further Scotland he ran hither to death; *let us also go and die with him.*[486] I must, I must tell that which of necessity I saw. The celebration, everywhere renowned, of All Saints comes, and according to the ancient saying, *Music in mourning is an unseasonable discourse.*[487] We come, we sing, even against our will. We weep while we sing and we sing while we weep. Malachy, though he sings not, yet does not lament. For why should he lament, who is drawing near to joy? For *us who remain,*[488] mourning remains. Malachy alone keeps festival. For what he cannot do with his body he does with his mind, as it is written, *The thought of man shall confess to thee, and the residue of thought shall keep the day of festival to thee.*[489] When the instrument of the body fails him, and the organ of the mouth is silent, and the office of the voice ceases, it remains that with songs in his heart he keeps festival. Why should not the saint keep festival, who is being brought to the festival of the

---

486 John xi. 16.
487 Ecclus. xxii. 6.
488 1 Thess. iv. 17.
489 Ps. lxxvi. 10 (vg.).

saints? He presents to them what will soon be due to himself. *Yet a little while*[490] and he will be one of them.

73. Towards the dusk of night, when now somehow the celebration of the day had been finished by us, Malachy had drawn near, not to dusk but to dawn. Was it not dawn to him[491] for whom *the night is far spent and the day is at hand*?[492] So, the fever increasing, a burning sweat from within him began to break out over his whole body, that, as it were *going through fire and through water, he might be brought into a wealthy place*.[493] Now his life was despaired of, now each one condemned his own judgement, now none doubted that Malachy's word was prevailing. We were called; we came. And lifting up his eyes on those who stood round him, he said, "*With desire I have desired to eat this passover* with *you*;[494] I give thanks to the divine compassion, I have *not been disappointed of my desire*."[495] Do you see the man free from care in death, and, not yet

490 John xiv. 19, etc.

491 Cp. *Cant.* xxvi. 11

492 Rom. xiii. 12.

493 Ps. lxvi. 12.

494 Luke xxii. 51.

495 Ps. lxxviii. 30 (vg.).

dead, already certain of life? No wonder. Seeing that the night was come to which he had looked forward, and that in it the day was dawning for him, so to speak triumphing over the night, he seemed to scoff at the darkness and as it were to cry, "*I shall* not *say, surely the darkness shall cover me*, because this *night shall be light about me in my pleasure*."[496] And tenderly consoling us he said, "Take care of me; if it be allowed me I shall not forget you. And it shall be allowed. *I have believed in God*,[497] and *all things are possible to him that believeth*.[498] I have loved God; I have loved you, and *charity never faileth*."[499] *And looking up to heaven*[500] he said, "O God, *keep them in Thy name*;[501] *and not these* only *but* all them *also who through* my *word*[502] and ministry have given themselves to thy service." Then, laying his hands on each one severally and blessing all, he bade them go to rest, *because his hour was not yet come*.[503]

---

496 Ps. cxxxix. 11 (vg.).
497 John xiv. 1.
498 Mark ix. 23.
499 1 Cor. xiii. 8.
500 Mark vii. 34.
501 John xvii. 11.
502 John xvii. 20.
503 John vii. 30.

74. We went. We returned about midnight, for at that hour it was announced that *the light shineth in darkness.*[504] The house filled, the whole community was present, many abbots also who had assembled. *With psalms and hymns and spiritual songs*[505] we followed our friend as he returned to his own country. In the fifty-fourth year of his age, at the place and time which he had chosen beforehand and predicted, Malachy, the bishop and legate of the holy Apostolic See, taken up *by the angels*,[506] as it were from our hands, happily *fell asleep in the Lord.*[507] And indeed he slept. His placid face was the sign of a placid departure. And verily *the eyes of all were* fixed *upon him*;[508] but none could perceive when he departed. When dead he was thought to be alive, when alive, dead; so true was it that there was no difference which might distinguish death from life. The same vivacity of face, the same serenity, as commonly appears in one who sleeps. You might say that death robbed him of none of these things, but rather very greatly increased them. He was not changed; but

---

504 John i. 5.

505 Eph. v. 19; Col. iii. 16.

506 Luke xvi. 22.

507 Acts vii. 60 (vg.).

508 Luke iv. 20.

he changed us all. In wondrous fashion the sorrow and groaning of all suddenly sank to rest, *sadness* was changed *into joy*,[509] singing banished lamentation.[510] He is borne forth, voices are borne to heaven, he is borne into the oratory on the shoulders of the abbots. *Faith has conquered*,[511] affection triumphs, things assume their normal course. All things are carried out in order, all proceed in the way of reason.

75. And in truth what reason is there to lament Malachy immoderately, as though his *death* was not *precious*,[512] as though it was not rather sleep than death, as though it was not the port of death and the portal of life? *Our friend* Malachy *sleepeth*;[513] and I, must I mourn? such mourning is based on custom, not on reason. If the Lord *hath given His beloved one sleep*, and such sleep, in which there is *an heritage of the Lord*, even *children, and the reward, the fruit of the womb*,[514] which of these things seems to call for weeping? Must I weep

---

509 Esth. xiii. 17 (vg.); xvi. 21 (vg.); cp. John xvi. 20, etc.

510 Cp. Amos viii. 10.

511 1 John v. 5.

512 Ps. cxvi. 15.

513 John xi. 11.

514 Ps. cxxvii. 2, 3 (vg.).

for him who has escaped from weeping? He rejoices, he triumphs, he has been brought *into the joy of his Lord*,[515] and I, must I lament for him? I desire these things for myself, I do not grudge them to him. Meanwhile the obsequies are prepared, the sacrifice is offered for him, all is performed according to custom with the greatest devotion. There stood some way off a boy whose arm hung by his side dead, rather burdensome to him than useful. When I discovered him I signed to him to come near, and taking his withered hand I laid it on the hand of the bishop, and it restored it to life. For in truth *the grace of healings*[516] lived in the dead; and his hand was to the dead hand what Elisha was to the dead man.[517] The boy *had come from far*[518] and the hand which he brought hanging down, he carried back whole to his own country. Now, all things having been duly accomplished in the very oratory of Saint Mary, Mother of God, *in which he was well pleased*,[519] Malachy is carried to his burial in the eleven hundred and forty-eighth year from the Incarnation of the Lord, on the fourth

---

515 Matt. xxv. 21, 23.

516 1 Cor. xii. 9 (vg.).

517 2 Kings xiii. 21.

518 Mark viii. 3.

519 Matt. iii. 17.

of the Nones of November. Thine, good Jesus, is *the deposit* which has been committed to us,[520] Thine is the treasure which is laid up with us. We *keep* it[521] to be given back at the time when Thou shalt see fit to recall it; only that he may not go forth without his comrades, but that him whom we have had as our guest we may have also as our leader, when we *shall reign* with Thee, and with him also, *for ever and ever*.[522] Amen.

520 2 Tim. i. 12.
521 2 Tim. i. 12.
522 Rev. xxii. 5.

Letters of St. Bernard

I

To Malachy. 1141.

(Epistle 341.)

To the venerable lord and most blessed father, Malachy, by the grace of God archbishop of the Irish, legate of the Apostolic See, Brother Bernard called to be abbot of Clairvaux, [desiring] to find grace with the Lord.

1. Amid the manifold *anxieties* and *cares* of my *heart*, by the multitude of which *my soul is sore vexed*,[523] the brothers *coming from a far country*[524] that they may serve the Lord, *thy* letter, *and thy staff, they comfort me*:[525] the letter, as a proof of good will; the staff, to support my

523 Ps. vi. 3.
524 Josh. ix. 6.
525 Ps. xxiii. 4.

weak body; the brothers, because they serve the Lord *in a humble spirit.* We have received them all, we are pleased with all, *all* alike *work together for good.*[526] But as to the wish that you have expressed that two of the brothers should be sent to look out a place for you beforehand, having taken counsel with the brothers, we have not thought it meet that they should be *separated one from another*[527] *until Christ be more fully formed in them,*[528] until they are wholly instructed in *the battles of the Lord.*[529] When therefore they have been taught in the school of the Holy Spirit, when they have been *endued with power from on high,*[530] then at length the sons shall return to their father that they may *sing the Lord's song,* not now *in a strange land,*[531] but in their own.

2. But do you yourselves in the mean time, according to *the wisdom given you*[532] by the Lord, look out

---

526 Rom. viii. 28.
527 Matt. xxv. 32.
528 Gal. iv. 19.
529 1 Sam. xxv. 28.
530 Luke xxiv. 49.
531 Ps. cxxxvii. 4.
532 2 Pet. iii. 15.

beforehand and *prepare* beforehand *a place for them*,[533] like the places which you have seen here, apart from the commotions of the world. *For the time is at hand*[534] when, by the operation of the grace of God, we shall bring forth for you *new men* out of the *old.*[535] *Blessed be the Name of the Lord for ever,*[536] *of whose only gift it cometh that* I have sons in common with you, whom your preaching *planted* and our exhortation *watered*, but *God gave the increase.*[537] We beseech your holiness to *preach the word of the Lord*[538] so that you may *give knowledge of salvation unto His people.*[539] *For* a double *necessity is laid upon you*,[540] both from your office as legate and your duty as bishop. Finally, since *in many things we offend all*,[541] and, being often thrown among the men of this age, we are much besmirched with the dust of the world, I commend myself to your prayers and to those of your companions, that in His fountain

---

533 John xiv. 2.

534 Rev. i. 3; xxii. 10.

535 Cp. Rom. vi. 6; Eph. ii. 15; iv. 22, 24.

536 Dan. ii. 20, etc.

537 1 Cor. iii. 6.

538 Acts xv. 36.

539 Luke i. 77.

540 1 Cor. ix. 16.

541 Jas. iii. 2.

of mercy Jesus Christ, himself the fountain of pity, may deign to wash and cleanse us, who said to Peter, *If I wash thee not, thou shalt have no part with me.*[542] And, indeed, I not only earnestly entreat this of you, but also require it as in some sense the payment of a debt, since I cry to the Lord for you, if the prayer of a sinner can do anything. Farewell in the Lord.

II

TO MALACHY. 1141 *or* 1142.

(Epistle 356.)

To Malachy, by the grace of God bishop, legate of the Apostolic See, Brother Bernard, called to be abbot of Clairvaux, if the prayer of a sinner can do anything, and if the devotion of a poor man is of any advantage.

We have done what your holiness commanded, not perhaps as it was worthy to be done, yet as well as was possible considering the time in which we live. So great evil everywhere struts about among us that it was scarcely possible to do the little that has been done. We have sent only a few grains of seed, as you see, to sow

542 John xiii. 8 (inexact quotation).

at least a small part of that *field* into which the true *Isaac* once went out *to meditate*, when *Rebekah* was first brought to him by Abraham's *servant*, to be happily joined to him in everlasting marriage.[543] And the seed is not to be despised concerning which we find that word fulfilled at this time in your regions, *Except the Lord of Sabaoth had left us a seed, we had been as Sodoma, and been made like unto Gomorrha.*[544] *I*, therefore, have sown, do you *water*, and *God shall give the increase.*[545] All the saints who are with you we salute through you, humbly commending ourselves to their holy prayers and yours. Farewell.

III

TO MALACHY. 1143 *or* 1144.

(Epistle 357.)

To our most loving father and most revered lord, Malachy, by the grace of God bishop, legate of the Holy and Apostolic See, the servant of his holiness, Brother

543 Gen. xxiv. 63 ff.

544 Rom. ix. 29 (inexact quotation).

545 1 Cor. iii. 6.

Bernard, called to be abbot of Clairvaux, health and our prayers, of whatever value they may be.

1. *How sweet are thy words unto my taste*,[546] my lord and father. How pleasant is *the remembrance of thy holiness*.[547] If there is any love, any devotedness, any good will in us, without doubt the charity of your belovedness claims it all as its due. There is no need for a multitude of words where affection blossoms abundantly. For I am confident that *the Spirit which* you have *from God*[548] bears *witness with your spirit that*[549] *what we are*,[550] however small it be, *is yours*.[551] You also, most loving and most longed-for father, *deliver not* to forgetfulness *the soul of the poor man*, which cleaves *to thee* with the bonds of charity, *and forget not the soul of thy poor man for ever*.[552] For neither, as it were anew, *do we commend ourselves unto you*[553] when now for a long

546 Ps. cxix. 103.
547 Ps. xxx. 4.
548 1 Cor. ii. 12.
549 Rom. viii. 16.
550 1 Cor xv. 10.
551 1 Cor. iii. 22.
552 Ps. lxxiv. 19 (vg.); Jer. xx. 13.
553 2 Cor. v. 12.

time we *glory in the Lord*[554] that our littleness has been worthy *to find grace in the sight of* your holiness;[555] but we pray that our affection, no longer new, may advance with new accessions day by day. We commend to you our sons, yea also yours, and the more earnestly because they are so far removed from us. You know that, after God, all our trust was in you, in sending them, because it seemed to us wrong not to fulfil the prayers of your holiness. See, as becomes you, that with your whole heart of love you embrace them and cherish them. In no wise for any cause let your earnest care for them grow cold, nor let that perish *which thy right hand hath planted.*[556]

2. We have now indeed learned both from your letter and from the report of our brothers that the house is making good progress, [and] is being enriched both in temporal and spiritual possessions. Wherefore we rejoice greatly with you and give thanks with our whole heart to God and to your fatherly care. And because there is still need of great watchfulness, because the place is new, and the land unaccustomed to the monastic life,

554 2 Cor. x. 17; 1 Cor. i. 31.

555 1 Sam. i. 18, etc.

556 Ps. lxxx. 15.

yea, without any experience of it, *we beseech you in the Lord,*[557] *that you slack not your hand,*[558] but perfectly accomplish that which you have well begun. Concerning our brothers who have returned from that place, it had pleased us well if they had remained. But perhaps the brothers of your country, whose characters are less disciplined and who have lent a less ready ear to advice in those observances, which were new to them, have been in some measure the reason for their return.

3. We have sent back to you Christian, our very dear son, and yours. We have instructed him more fully, as far as we could, in the things which belong to the [Cistercian] Order, and henceforth, as we hope, he will be more careful concerning its obligations. Do not be surprised that we have not sent any other brothers with him; for we did not find competent brothers who were ready to assent to our wishes, and it was not our plan to compel the unwilling. Our much-loved brother, Robert, assented on this occasion also to our prayers, *as an obedient son.*[559] It will be your part to assist him that your house may now be set forward, both in build-

557 1 Thess. iv. 1.

558 Josh. x. 6.

559 1 Pet. i. 14 (vg., inexact quotation).

ings and in other necessaries. This also we suggest to your fatherhood, that you persuade religious men and those who, you hope, will be useful to the monastery, to come into their Order, for this will be of the greatest advantage to the house, and to you they will pay the greater heed. May your holiness have good health, being always mindful of us in Christ.

IV

TO THE BROTHERS IN IRELAND. November 1148.

(Epistle 374.)

To the religious brothers who are in Ireland, and especially to those communities which Malachy the bishop, of blessed memory, founded, Brother Bernard, called to be abbot of Clairvaux, [wishing them] *the consolation of the Comforter.*[560]

1. If *here we had a continuing city* we should rightly mourn with most abundant tears that we had lost such a fellow-citizen. But if *we* rather *seek one to come,*[561] as befits us, it is nevertheless no small cause of grief that

560 Acts ix. 31, combined with John xiv. 26, etc.

561 Heb. xiii. 14.

we are bereaved of a guide so indispensable. We ought, however, to regulate passion with knowledge and to mitigate grief with the *confidence of hope*.[562] Nor does it become any one to wonder if love compels groaning, if desolation draws forth tears: yet we must set a limit to these things, nay in no small measure be consoled while we gaze *not at the things which are seen, but at the things which are not seen; for the things which are seen are temporal, but the things which are not seen are eternal.*[563] First, indeed, we ought to rejoice with the holy soul, lest he accuse us of want of charity, saying also himself what the Lord said to the apostles, "*If ye loved me ye would rejoice because I go unto the Father.*"[564] The spirit of our father has gone before us to *the Father of spirits*,[565] and we are convicted, not only as wanting in charity, but even as guilty of ingratitude for all the benefits which came to us through him, if we do not rejoice with him who has *departed* from labour to rest, from danger to safety, from *the world unto the Father*.[566] Therefore, if it is an act of filial piety to weep for Mal-

562 Cp. Heb. iii. 6.

563 2 Cor. iv. 18.

564 John xiv. 28.

565 Heb. xii. 9.

566 John xiii. 1.

achy who is dead, yet more is it an act of piety to rejoice with Malachy who is alive. Is he not alive? Assuredly he is, and in bliss. *In the eyes of the foolish he seemed to have died; but he is in peace.*

2. Hence even the thought of our own advantage provides us with another motive for great joy and gladness, because so powerful a patron, so faithful an advocate has gone before us to the heavenly court. For his most fervent charity cannot forget his sons, and his approved holiness must secure *favour with God.*[567] For who would dare to suppose that this holy Malachy can now be less profitable [than before] or less loving to his own? Assuredly, if he was loved aforetime, now he receives from God surer proofs of His love, and *having loved his own, he loved them unto the end.*[568] Far be it from us, holy soul, to esteem thy prayer now less effectual, for now thou canst make supplication with more vigour in the presence of *the Majesty*[569] and thou no longer *walkest in faith*, but reignest *in the sight* of Him.[570] Far be it from us to count that laborious charity of thine as dimin-

567 Luke ii. 52.

568 John xiii. 1 (inexact quotation).

569 Heb. i. 3.

570 2 Cor. v. 7 (inexact quotation).

ished, not to say made void, now that thou prostratest thyself at the very fountain of eternal charity, quaffing full draughts of that for the very drops of which thou didst thirst before. Charity, *strong as death*,[571] yea even stronger than death itself, could not yield to death. For even at the moment of his departure he was not unmindful of you, with exceptional affection commending you to God, and with his accustomed *meekness and lowliness*[572] praying our insignificance also that we should not *forget you for ever*.[573] Wherefore also we thought good to write to you that you may know that we are ready to bestow upon you all consolation with entire devotion, whether in spiritual things, if in them our insignificance can ever do anything by the merits of this our blessed father, or in temporal, if ever perchance opportunity should be given us.

3. And now also, dearly beloved, we are filled with heartfelt pity for this grievous bereavement of the Irish Church. And we unite ourselves the more with you in suffering because we know that by this very thing we have become the more your debtors. For the *Lord*

---

571 Cant. viii. 6.

572 Cp. Eph. iv. 2.

573 Ps. lxxiv, 19.

did great things for us[574] when He deigned to honour this place of ours by making it the scene of his blessed death, and to enrich it with the most costly treasure of his body. But do not take it ill that he is buried among us; for God so ordered, *according to the multitude of His mercies*,[575] that you should possess him in life, and that it might be allowed to us to possess him, if only in death. And to us, indeed, in common with you, he was, and still is, father. *For* even *in* his *death* this *testament was confirmed* to us.[576] Wherefore as, for the sake of so great a father, we embrace you all as our true brothers, with the unstinted yearning of charity, so also concerning yourselves, spiritual kinship persuades us that you are like-minded.

4. But we exhort you, brothers, that you be always careful to *walk in the steps of* this *our* blessed *father*,[577] by so much the more zealously as by daily proofs his *holy conversation*[578] was more certainly known to you. For in this you shall prove yourselves to be his true sons, if

574 Ps. cxxvi. 3.

575 Ps. cvi. 45.

576 Heb. ix. 17 (vg., inexact quotation).

577 Rom. iv. 12.

578 2 Pet. iii. 11.

you manfully maintain the father's ordinances, and if, as you have seen in him, and heard *from him how you ought to walk, you so walk that you may abound more and more*:[579] for the glory of a father is the wisdom of his sons.[580] For even for us the example of so great perfection in our midst has begun in no slight degree both to expel our sloth and impel us to reverence. And would that he may in such wise *draw us after him* that he may draw us to the goal, *running* more eagerly and more quickly in *the fragrance* which his virtues have left so fresh behind them.[581] May Christ guard all of you *while you pray for us*.[582]

579 1 Thess. iv. 1 (vg.).
580 Cp. Prov. x. 1.
581 Cant. i. 3, 4.
582 Col. iv. 3.

Sermons of St. Bernard on the Passing of Malachy

Sermon I

(November 2, 1148.)

1. A certain abundant blessing, dearly beloved, has been sent by the counsel of heaven to you this day; and if it were not faithfully divided, you would suffer loss, and I, to whom of a surety this office seems to have been committed, would incur danger. I fear therefore your loss, I fear my own damnation, if perchance it be said, *The young children ask bread, and no man offereth it unto them.*[583] For I know how necessary for you is the consolation which comes from heaven, since it is certain that you have manfully renounced carnal

583 Lam. iv. 4 (inexact quotation).

delights and worldly pleasures. None can reasonably doubt that it was by the good gift of heaven, and *determined by* divine *purpose*,[584] that Bishop Malachy should fall asleep among you today, and among you have his place of burial, as he desired. For if not even a leaf of a tree *falls* to *the ground without* the will of God,[585] who is so dull as not to see plainly in the coming of this blessed man, and his passing, a truly great purpose of the divine compassion? *From the uttermost parts of the earth he came*[586] to leave his earth here. He was hastening, it is true, on another errand; but we know that by reason of his special love for us he desired that most of all. He suffered many hindrances in the journey itself, and he was refused permission to cross the sea till the time of his consummation was drawing near, and the goal which could not be passed. And when, with many labours, he came to us *we received him as an angel of God*[587] out of reverence for his holiness; but he, out of his very deeply rooted *meekness and lowliness*,[588] far beyond our merits, received us with devoted love. Then

584 Acts ii. 23.

585 Cp. Matt. x. 29.

586 Matt. xii. 42.

587 Gal. iv. 14 (inexact quotation).

588 Cp. Eph. iv. 2.

he spent a few days with us in his usual health: for he was waiting for his companions, who had been scattered in England, when the baseless distrust of the king was hindering the man of God. And when they had all assembled to him, he was preparing to set out to the Roman Court, on his way to which he had come hither; when suddenly he was overtaken by sickness, and he immediately perceived that he was being summoned rather to the heavenly palace, *God having provided some better thing for us*, lest going out from *us he should be made perfect* elsewhere.[589]

2. There appeared to the physicians no sign in him, I say not of death, but even of serious illness; but he, gladdened in spirit, said that in every way it was befitting that this year Malachy should depart from this life. We laboured to prevent it, both by earnest prayers to God, and by whatever other means we could; but his merits prevailed, that *his heart's desire should be given him and* that *the request of his lips* should *not be withholden.*[590] For so all things happened to him in accordance with his wishes; that by the inspiration of the divine goodness he had chosen this place above all others, and that

589 Heb. xi. 40.

590 Ps. xxi. 2.

he had long desired that he should have as the day of his burial this day on which the general memory of all the faithful is celebrated. Moreover, these joys of ours were worthily increased by the circumstance that we had selected that same day, by God's will, for bringing hither from the former cemetery for their second burial the bones of our brothers. And when we were bringing them, and singing psalms in the accustomed manner, the same holy man said that he was very greatly delighted with that chanting. And not long after, he himself also followed, having sunk into a most sweet and blessed sleep. Therefore we render thanks to God for all the things that He has disposed, because He willed to honour us, unworthy as we are, by his blessed death among us, to enrich His poor with the most costly treasure of his body, and to strengthen us, who are weak, by so great a *pillar*[591] of His church. For one or other of two *signs* proves that it was *wrought for us for good*,[592] either that this place is pleasing to God, or that it is His will to make it pleasing to Him, since He led to it *from the uttermost parts of the earth*[593] so holy a man to die and to be buried there.

591 Gal. ii. 9.

592 Ps. lxxxvi. 17 (vg.).

593 Matt. xii. 42.

3. But our very love for this blessed father compels us to sorrow with that people from our heart, and to shudder exceedingly at the cruelty of him, even Death, who has not spared to inflict this terrible wound on the Church, now so much to be pitied. Terrible and unpitying surely is death, which has punished so great a multitude of men by smiting one; blind and without foresight, which has tied the tongue of Malachy, arrested his steps, relaxed his hands, closed his eyes. Those devout eyes, I say, which were wont to restore divine grace to sinners, by most tender tears; those most holy *hands*, which had always loved to be occupied in laborious and humble deeds, which so often *offered for* sinners *the saving sacrifice*[594] of the Lord's body, and were *lifted up* to heaven in prayer *without wrath and doubting*,[595] which are known to have bestowed many benefits on the sick and to have been resplendent with manifold signs; those *beautiful* steps also of *him that preached the Gospel of peace and brought glad tidings of good things*; those *feet*,[596] which were so often wearied with eagerness to show pity; those footprints which were always

594 2 Macc. iii. 32 (vg.).

595 1 Tim. ii. 8.

596 Rom. x. 15.

worthy to merit devout kisses;[597] finally, those holy *lips of the priest*, which *kept knowledge*,[598] *the mouth of the righteous*, which *spoke wisdom, and his tongue* which, *talking of judgement*,[599] yea *and of mercy*,[600] was wont to heal so great wounds of souls. And it is no wonder, brothers, that *death* is iniquitous, since iniquity *brought* it *forth*,[601] that it is heedless, since it is known to have been born of *seduction*.[602] It is nothing wonderful, I say, if it strikes without distinction, since it came from *the transgression*;[603] if it is cruel and mad, since it was produced by the subtlety of *the old serpent*[604] and the folly of the woman. But why do we charge against it that it dared to assail Malachy, a faithful *member*, it is true, *of Christ*,[605] when it also rushed madly upon the very *head* of[606] Malachy and of all the elect as well? It rushed, assuredly, upon One whom it could not hurt; but it

597 Cp. Luke vii. 38.
598 Mal. ii. 7.
599 Ps. xxxvii. 30.
600 Ps. ci. 1.
601 Jas. i. 15.
602 Cp. 2 Cor. xi. 3; 1 Tim. ii. 14.
603 1 Tim. ii. 14.
604 Rev. xii. 9; xx. 2.
605 1 Cor. vi. 15, etc.
606 Eph. iv. 15, etc.

did not rush away unhurt. Death hurled itself against life, and life shut up death within itself, and *death* was *swallowed up of life.*[607] Gulping down the hook to its hurt, it began to be held by Him whom it seemed to have held.[608]

4. But perhaps someone may say, How does it appear that death has been overcome by the Head, if it still rages with so great liberty against the members? If death is dead, how did it kill Malachy? If it is conquered how has it still power over all, and *there is no man that liveth and shall not see death*?[609] Death is clearly conquered—*the work of the devil*[610] and the penalty of sin: sin is conquered, the cause of death; and *the wicked one* himself is *conquered,*[611] the author both of sin and death. And not only are these things conquered, they are, moreover, already judged and condemned. The sentence is determined, but not yet published. In fact, *the fire is prepared for the devil,*[612] though he is not yet

---

607 1 Cor. xv. 54, combined with 2 Cor. v. 4.

608 Cp. *Cant.* xxvi. 11.

609 Ps. lxxxix. 48 (vg.).

610 1 John iii. 8.

611 1 John ii. 13, 14.

612 Matt. xxv. 41.

cast into the fire, though still for *a short time*[613] he is allowed to work wickedness. He is become, as it were, the hammer of the Heavenly Workman, *the hammer of the whole earth.*[614] He crushes the elect *for* their *profit*,[615] he crushes to powder the reprobate for their damnation. As is the *master of the house*, so are *they of his household*,[616] that is, sin and death. For *sin*, though it is not to be doubted that it was *nailed* with Christ *to His cross*,[617] was yet allowed still for a time, *not* indeed to *reign*,[618] but to dwell even in the Apostle himself while he lived. I lie if he does not himself say, *It is no more I that do it, but sin dwelleth in me.*[619] So also death itself is by no means, indeed, yet compelled not to be present, but it is compelled not to be present to men's hurt. But there will come a time when it is said, *O death, where is thy victory?*[620] For death also is *the last enemy that shall be destroyed.*[621] But now, since He rules

613 Rev. xii. 12.
614 Jer. l. 23.
615 1 Cor. xii. 7 (vg.).
616 Matt. x. 25.
617 Col. ii. 14.
618 Rom. vi. 12.
619 Rom. vii. 17.
620 1 Cor. xv. 55 (vg.).
621 1 Cor. xv. 26.

who has the power of life and *death*[622] and confines the very sea within the fixed limits of its shores, death itself to the beloved of the Lord is a sleep of refreshment. The prophet bears witness who says, *When he giveth his beloved sleep, behold the heritage of the Lord.*[623] *The death of the wicked is indeed most evil,*[624] since their birth is evil and their life more evil; but *precious is the death of the saints.*[625] Precious clearly, for it is the end of labours, the consummation of victory, the gate of life, and the entrance to perfect safety.

5. Let us rejoice therefore, brothers, let us rejoice as is meet, with our father, for if it is an act of filial piety to mourn for Malachy who is dead, yet more is it an act of piety to rejoice with Malachy who is alive. Is he not alive? He is, and in bliss. Certainly, *in the eyes of the foolish he seemed to have died; but he is in peace.*[626] In fine, *now a fellow-citizen with the saints, and of the household of God,*[627] he at once sings and gives thanks,

---

622 Heb. ii. 14; Tobit ii. 8.
623 Ps. cxxvii. 2, 3 (vg.).
624 Ps. xxxiv. 21 (vg.).
625 Ps. cxvi. 15.
626 Wisd. iii. 2, 3.
627 Eph. ii. 19 (with variant).

saying, *We went through fire and water; but thou broughtest us out into a wealthy place.*[628] He *went*, clearly, in manly fashion, and he *went through*[629] happily. The true Hebrew celebrated the Passover in spirit, and as he went, he said to us, "*With desire I have desired to eat this Passover with you.*"[630] *He went through fire and water*,[631] whom neither experiences of sadness could crush, nor pleasures hold back. For there is below us a place which fire wholly claims as its own, so that the wretched Dives could not have there even the least drop of *water* from the *finger* of *Lazarus*.[632] There is also above *the city of God* which *the streams of the river make glad*,[633] *a torrent of pleasure*,[634] *a cup which inebriates, how goodly*![635] Here, *in the midst*, truly is found *the knowledge of good and evil*,[636] and in this place we may receive the *trial* of pleasure and *of affliction*.[637] Unhappy Eve

628 Ps. lxvi. 12.
629 Hos. x. 15 (vg.: xi. 1).
630 Luke xxii. 15.
631 Ps. lxvi. 12.
632 Luke xvi. 24, 25.
633 Ps. xlvi. 4.
634 Ps. xxxvi. 8 (vg.).
635 Ps. xxiii. 5 (vg.).
636 Gen. ii. 9.
637 2 Cor. viii. 2.

brought us into these alternations. Here clearly is day and night; for in the lower world there is only night, and in heaven only day.[638] Blessed is the soul which passes through both, neither ensnared by pleasure nor *fainting at tribulation.*[639]

6. I think it right to relate to you, briefly, a specimen of the many splendid deeds of this man, in which he is known to have *gone*, with no little vigour, *through fire and water.*[640] A tyrannous race laid claim to the metropolitan see of Patrick, the great apostle of the Irish, creating archbishops in regular succession, and *possessing the sanctuary of God by hereditary right.*[641] Our Malachy was therefore asked by the faithful to combat such great evils; and *putting his life in his hand*[642] he advanced to the attack with vigour, he undertook the archbishopric, exposing himself to evident danger, that he might put an end to so great a crime. Surrounded by perils he ruled the church; when the perils were passed, immediately he canonically ordained another

638 Rev. xxi. 25; xxii. 5.

639 Eph. iii. 13.

640 Ps. lxvi. 12.

641 Ps. lxxxiii 12 (vg.).

642 1 Sam. xix. 5.

as his successor. For he had undertaken the office on this condition, that when the fury of persecution had ceased and it thus became possible that another should safely be appointed, he should be allowed to return to his own see. And there, without ecclesiastical or secular revenues he lived in the religious communities which he himself had formed, dwelling among them up to this time as one of themselves, and abjuring all personal property. So the fire of *affliction tried*[643] the man of God, but did not consume him; for he was gold. So neither did pleasure hold him captive or destroy him, nor did he stand a curious spectator on the way, forgetful of his own pilgrimage.

7. Which of you, brothers, would not earnestly desire to imitate his holiness, if he dared even to hope for such an attainment? I believe, therefore, you will gladly hear, if I perchance can tell it, what made Malachy holy. But lest our testimony should seem not easy to be received, hear what the Scripture says: *He made him holy in his faith and meekness.*[644] By faith he trampled on the world, as John bears witness when he says, *This is the victory*

643 Ps. lxvi. 10, 11.

644 Ecclus. xlv. 4 (vg.).

that overcometh the world, even our faith.[645] For *in the spirit of meekness*[646] he endured all things whatsoever that were hard and contrary with *good cheer.*[647] On the one hand, indeed, after the example of Christ, by faith he trampled on the seas,[648] lest he should be entangled in pleasures; on the other, *in his patience he possessed his soul,*[649] lest he should be crushed by troubles. For concerning these two things you have the saying in the Psalm, *A thousand shall fall at thy side, and ten thousand at thy right hand;*[650] for many more are cast down by the deceitfulness of prosperity than by the lashes of adversity. Therefore, dearly beloved, let none of us, allured by the level surface of the easier way, suppose that road of the sea to be more convenient for himself. This plain has great mountains, invisible indeed, but for that very reason more dangerous. That way perhaps seems more laborious which passes through the steeps of the hills and the ruggedness of rocks; but to them that have tried it, it is found far safer and more to be desired.

---

645 1 John v. 4.

646 Gal. vi. 1.

647 1 Kings xxi. 7 (vg.).

648 Cp. Matt. xiv. 25; John vi. 19.

649 Luke xxi. 19.

650 Ps. xci. 7.

But on both sides there is labour, on both sides danger, as he knew who said, *By the armour of righteousness on the right hand and on the left*;[651] so that we may rightly rejoice with those that *went through fire and water and have been brought into a wealthy place*.[652] Do you wish to hear something about the *wealthy place*? Would that another might speak to you of it. For as for me, that which I have not tasted I cannot indite.

8. But I seem to hear Malachy saying to me today about this *wealthy place*, *Return unto thy rest, O my soul; for the Lord hath dealt bountifully with thee: for he hath delivered my soul from death, [mine eyes from tears, and my feet from falling]*.[653] And what I understand to be expressed in those words hear in a few sentences; *for the day is far spent*,[654] and I have spoken at greater length than I intended, because I am unwilling to tear myself away from the sweetness of the father's name, and my tongue, dreading to be silent about Malachy, fears to cease. The death of the soul,[655] my brothers, is sin; unless

651 2 Cor. vi. 7.

652 Ps. lxvi. 12.

653 Ps. cxvi. 7, 8 (vg.).

654 Luke xxiv. 29.

655 Cp. Ps. cxvi. 8.

you have overlooked that which you have read in the prophet: *The soul that sinneth, it shall die.*[656] Threefold, then, is the rejoicing of the man, since he is delivered from all sin, and from labour, and from danger. For from this time neither is *sin* said to *dwell in him*,[657] nor is the sorrow of penitence enjoined, nor from henceforth is he warned to guard himself *from* any *falling*.[658] *Elijah* has laid aside his *mantle*;[659] it was not that he feared, it was not that he was afraid that it should be touched, still less *retained*, by an adulteress.[660] He went up into the *chariot*;[661] he is not now in terror of falling; he mounts delightfully; he labours not to fly by his own power, but sits in a swift vehicle. To this *wealthy place*, dearly beloved, *let us run* with all eagerness of spirit, in *the fragrance of the ointments* of this our blessed father, who this day has been seen to have stirred up our torpor to most fervent desire. Let us run after him, I say, crying to him again and again, "*Draw us after thee*";[662]

---

656 Ezek. xviii. 4.

657 Rom. vii. 17, 20.

658 Ps. cxvi. 8.

659 2 Kings ii. 13.

660 Gen. xxxix. 12, 15 (vg.).

661 2 Kings ii. 11.

662 Cant. i. 3, 4.

and, with earnest heart and advancing holiness of life, returning devout thanks to the Almighty Pity, that He has willed that His unworthy servants, who are without merits of their own, should at least not be without the prayers of another.

SERMON II

(November 2, 1149)

1. It is clear, dearly beloved, *that whilst we are* detained *in the body we are absent from the Lord.*[663] And throughout this wretched time of detention banishment and conscience of faults enjoins upon us sorrow rather than joy. But because by the mouth of the apostle we are exhorted to *rejoice with them that do rejoice*,[664] the time and the occasion require that we should be stirred up to all gladness. For if it is true, as the prophet perceived, that *the righteous rejoice before God*,[665] without doubt Malachy rejoices, who *in his days*[666] *pleased God*[667] and

663 2 Cor. v. 6.
664 Rom. xii. 15.
665 Ps. lxviii. 3.
666 Ecclus. xliv. 7.
667 Ecclus. xliv. 16 (vg.).

was found righteous.[668] Malachy ministered in *holiness and righteousness before Him*:[669] the ministry pleased Him; the minister also pleased Him. Why should he not please Him? He *made the Gospel without charge*,[670] he filled the country with the Gospel, he tamed the deathly barbarism of his Irishmen, with the *sword of the spirit*[671] he subdued foreign nations to the *light yoke* of Christ,[672] *restoring His inheritance to Him*[673] *even unto the ends of the earth.*[674] O, fruitful ministry! O, faithful minister! Is not the promise of the Father to the Son fulfilled through him? Did not the Father behold him long ago when He said to the Son, *I shall give thee the heathen for thine inheritance, and the uttermost parts of the earth for thy possession.*[675] How willingly the Saviour received what He had *bought*,[676] and had *bought with*

668 Ecclus. xliv. 17.
669 Luke i. 75.
670 1 Cor. ix. 18.—Cp.
671 Eph. vi. 17.
672 Matt. xi. 30.
673 Ps. xvi. 5 (vg.).
674 Isa. xlviii. 20; Jer. xxv. 31.
675 Ps. ii. 8.
676 2 Pet. ii. 1.

the price[677] of *His own blood*,[678] with the shame of the Cross, with the horror of the Passion. How willingly from the hands of Malachy, because he ministered *freely*.[679] So in the minister the freely executed office was acceptable, and in the ministry the conversion of sinners was pleasing. Acceptable and pleasing, I say, in the minister was the *singleness of eye*,[680] but in the ministry *the salvation of the people*.[681]

2. However, even though a less effective result of the ministry followed, He would nevertheless justly have had regard to Malachy and his works, He to whom purity is a friend and single-mindedness one of his household, to whose righteousness it belongs to weigh the work in accordance with its purpose, from the character of *the eye* to measure the state of *the whole body*.[682] But now *the works of the Lord are great, sought out according to all* the *desires*[683] and efforts of Malachy;

---

677 1 Cor. vi. 20.

678 Acts xx. 28.

679 2 Cor. xi. 7.

680 Matt. vi. 22; Luke xi. 34.

681 Hab. iii. 13.

682 Matt. vi. 22, 23; Luke xi. 34, 35.

683 Ps. cxi. 2 (vg.).

they are great and many and *very good*,[684] though better in proportion to the good origin of the pure purpose. What work of piety escaped the attention of Malachy? He was poor as regards himself, but rich to the poor. He was a *father of the fatherless*, a husband *of the widows*,[685] a protector of the oppressed. *A cheerful giver*,[686] seldom making petitions, modest in receiving gifts. He was specially solicitous, and had much success, in restoring peace between those who were at variance. Who was as tender as he in sharing the sufferings of others? who as ready to help? who as free in rebuke? For he was zealous, and yet not wanting in knowledge, the restrainer of zeal. And, indeed, *to the weak* he was *weak*,[687] but none the less strong to the strong: he *resisted the proud*,[688] he lashed the tyrants, a teacher of kings and princes. It was he who by prayer deprived a king of sight when he worked wickedness, and restored it when he was humbled. It was he, when certain men broke a peace which he had made, who gave them up

---

684 Gen. i. 31.

685 Ps. lxviii. 5.

686 2 Cor. ix. 7.

687 1 Cor. ix. 22.

688 Jas. iv. 6; 1 Pet. v. 5.

to *the spirit of error*,[689] and foiled them in the evil which they devised to do; and who compelled them to accept peace a second time, confounded and stunned by that which had happened to them. It was he to whom a river most opportunely lent its aid against the others, who were equally *transgressors of a covenant.*[690] In wonderful fashion, by throwing itself before them, it made void the efforts of the ungodly. There had been no rains, no floods of waters, no gathering of clouds, no melting of snows, when suddenly the mere rivulet was converted into a great river; and it rushed along and swelling up overflowed the banks, and utterly denied passage to those who wished to do wickedly.

3. What things we have heard and known of the wrath of the man and his vengeance on his enemies, while yet he was *sweet and gentle and plenteous in mercy unto all*[691] that suffered need! For he lived for all as though he were the one parent of all. *As a hen her chickens,*[692] so he cherished all and *protected them under the covert*

689 1 John iv. 6.

690 Josh. vii. 15, etc.

691 Ps. lxxxvi. 5 (vg.).

692 Matt. xxiii. 37.

of his wings.[693] He made no distinction of sex or age, of condition or person; he failed none, his loving heart embraced all. In whatsoever affliction men cried to him he counted it his own: even more than that, for in regard to his own afflictions he was patient, in regard to those of others he was compassionate, very often even passionate. For indeed sometimes, filled with wrath, he was stirred to take the part of one against another, that by *delivering the poor* and restraining the *strong*[694] he might take thought in equal measure for the salvation of all. Therefore he was angry; but it was in order that he might not sin by not being angry, according to the words of the Psalm, *Be ye angry and sin not.*[695] Anger did not rule him, but he himself *ruled his spirit.*[696] He had power over himself. Assuredly he who had the victory over himself could not be *mastered by anger.*[697] His anger was kept in hand. When it was summoned it came, going forth, not bursting forth; it was brought into action by his will, not by impulse. He was not set on fire by it, but used it. As well in this as in ruling

---

693 Ps. lxi. 4 (vg.).

694 Ps. xxxv. 10

695 Ps. iv. 4 (vg.).

696 Prov. xvi. 32.

697 Job xxxvi. 18 (vg.).

and restraining all the motions both of his inner and his outer man his judgement was careful, his caution great. For he did not give so much attention to all, as to leave himself alone out of account, as, in his universal solicitude, to disregard only himself. He was careful of himself also. He *guarded himself*.[698] In fact, he was so wholly his own, so wholly also belonged to all, that his love seemed in no degree to hinder or delay him from his guardianship of himself, nor his concern for his own person from the common good. If you saw the man busied in the midst of crowds, involved in cares, you would say he was born for his country, *not for himself*. If you saw the man alone and dwelling by himself, you would suppose that he lived for God alone and for himself.

4. Without tumult he went about among tumults; without ease he spent the time which he gave to ease. How could he be taking his ease when he *was occupied in the statutes of the Lord*?[699] For though he had time free from the necessities of the peoples, yet had he none unoccupied by holy meditations, by the work of prayer, by the ease itself of contemplation. In the time

---

698 1 Tim. v. 22.

699 Ps. cxix. 23.

of ease he spoke gravely or not at all. His mien was either courteous, or humble and self-restrained. Assuredly—a trait which is counted worthy of much praise among the wise—*his eye was in his head*,[700] never flying forth except when it was obedient to power. His laughter displayed love, or provoked it: but even so it was rare. Sometimes indeed, it came forth, but it was never forced, intimating the gladness of his heart in such a way that his mouth did not lose but gained in grace.[701] So modest was it that it could not be suspected of levity; so gentle, however, that it sufficed to free his joyous countenance from every trace and shadow of sadness. O perfect gift! O *rich burnt sacrifice*![702] O pleasing service in mind and hand! How *sweet unto God is the savour*[703] of him who employs his leisure in prayers, how sweet unto men of him who is occupied in fatiguing labours.

5. Because he was such an one, then, *beloved of God*[704] and men, not undeservedly was Malachy received this day into the company of angels, having attained in fact

700 Eccles. ii. 14 (inexact quotation).
701 Cp. Luke iv. 22.
702 Ps. xx. 3 (vg.).
703 2 Cor. ii. 15.
704 1 Thess. i. 4 (vg.); 2 Thess. ii. 13.

what his name denoted. And indeed, already he was an angel not less in purity than in name. But now more happily is the significance of his glorious name fulfilled in him, since he is glad with a glory and happiness equal to that of the angels. Let us also, dearly beloved, be glad because our *angel ascended*[705] to his fellow-citizens, acting as an ambassador for *the children of the captivity*,[706] winning for us the favour of the blessed ones, declaring to them the desires of the wretched. Let us *be glad*, I say, *and rejoice*,[707] because in that heavenly court there is one who went forth from us to take care of us, to protect us by his merits, whom he instructed by his example and strengthened by his miracles.

6. The holy pontiff, who *in a humble spirit* often brought peace-offerings to the heavens, today in his own person has *gone unto the altar of God*,[708] himself the victim and the priest. With the departure of the priest the rite of sacrifice is changed into a better thing. The *fountain of tears*[709] is dried up, every burnt sacrifice

---

705 Judg. xiii. 20.

706 Dan. vi. 13; Ezra iv. 1.

707 Ps. ix. 2.

708 Ps. xliii. 4.

709 Jer. ix. 1.

is made *with gladness and rejoicing.*[710] *Blessed be the Lord God of* Malachy, who by the ministry of so great a pontiff *hath visited his people,*[711] and now, *taking him up into the holy city,*[712] ceaseth not, by the remembrance of so great sweetness to *comfort our captivity.*[713] Let *the spirit of* Malachy *rejoice in the Lord,*[714] because he is freed from the heavy load of the body, and is no longer hindered, by the weight of impure and earthly matter, from passing with all eagerness and fullness of life, through the whole creation, corporeal and incorporeal, that he may enter entirely into God, and *joined to* Him may with Him *be one spirit*[715] for ever.

7. *Holiness becometh* that *house*[716] in *which the remembrance of* so great *holiness*[717] is celebrated. Holy Malachy, preserve it *in holiness and righteousness*[718] pitying us who in the midst of so many and great miseries

710 Ps. xlv. 15.
711 Luke i. 68.
712 Matt. iv. 5.
713 Ps. cxxvi. 1, 4 (vg.).
714 Luke i. 47.
715 1 Cor. vi. 17.
716 Ps. xciii. 5.
717 Ps. xxx. 4.
718 Luke i. 75.

utter the memory of thine abundant goodness.[719] Great is the dispensation of the mercy of God upon thee, who made thee *little in thine own sight,*[720] great in His; who *did* great things by thee, in saving thy country, *great things to thee,*[721] in bringing thee into His glory. May thy festival, which is deservedly devoted to thy virtues, have a saving efficacy for us by thy merits and prayers. *May the glory of thy holiness,*[722] which is celebrated by us, be continued by angels: so shall it meetly be pleasant for us, if it be also fruitful. While thou departest be it allowed to us, who are met together today in thy so delicious feast, to preserve some remnants of the fruits of the Spirit, loaded with which thou ascendest.

8. Be to us, we beseech thee, holy Malachy, another Moses, or another Elijah, like them imparting *of thy spirit*[723] to us, for thou hast come *in* their *spirit and power.*[724] Thy life was *a law of life and knowledge,*[725] thy death the port of death and the portal of life, thy mem-

719 Ps. cxlv. 7 (vg.).
720 1 Sam. xv. 17 (inexact quotation).
721 Luke i. 49.
722 Ps. cxlv. 5 (vg.).
723 Num. xi. 25; 2 Kings ii. 9, 15.
724 Luke i. 17.
725 Ecclus. xlv. 5.

ory the delight of sweetness and grace, thy presence *a crown of glory in the hand of the Lord*[726] thy God. O *fruitful olive tree in the house of God*![727] O *oil of gladness*,[728] giving both anointing and light, cherishing with favours, *resplendent with miracles*, make us partakers of that light and graciousness which thou enjoyest. O sweet-smelling *lily, blossoming and budding* evermore before the Lord, and spreading everywhere a *sweet* and life-giving *savour*,[729] *whose memorial is blessed*[730] with us, whose presence is in honour with those who are above, grant to those who sing of thee that they may not be deprived of their share in so great *an assembly*.[731] O *great luminary*[732] and *light* that *shinest in darkness*,[733] illuminating the prison, *making glad the city*[734] by the rays of thy signs and merits, by the lustre of virtues put to flight from our hearts the darkness of vices. O *morn-*

726 Isa. lxii. 3.

727 Ps. lii. 8 (vg.).

728 Ps. xlv. 7 (vg.).

729 Isa. xxvii. 6, combined with Hos. xiv. 5, and Ecclus. xxxix. 14.

730 Ecclus. xlv. 1.

731 Ecclus. xxiv. 2, 12 (vg.).

732 Ps. cxxxvi. 7.

733 John i. 4.

734 Ps. xlvi. 4.

ing star,[735] more brilliant than the rest because thou art nearer the day, more like to the sun, deign to go before us, that we also may *walk in the light as children of light*, and *not* children *of darkness*.[736] O thou who art the dawn breaking into day upon the earth, but *the noon light*[737] illumining the higher regions of heaven, receive us in the fellowship of light, by which illuminated thou sheddest light far without, and sweetly burnest within, by the gift of our Lord Jesus Christ, who with the Father and the Holy Spirit reigneth One God, world without end.—AMEN.

---

735 Ecclus. l. 6.

736 1 John i. 7, combined with 1 Thess. v. 5.

737 Isa. xviii. 4 (vg.).